WE ARE TALKING ABOUT HOMES

Also by Lynne Sharon Schwartz

Rough Strife

Balancing Acts

Disturbances in the Field

Acquainted with the Night

We Are Talking About Homes

A Great University Against Its Neighbors

Lynne Sharon Schwartz

1817
HARPER & ROW, PUBLISHERS, New York
Cambridge, Philadelphia, San Francisco, London
Mexico City, São Paulo, Singapore, Sydney

Grateful acknowledgment is made for permission to reprint "Tribute from a Neighbor," by Eve Merriam, which originally appeared in *Equity* magazine, 1968.

 For information address Harper & Row, Publishers, Inc., 10 East 53rd Street, New York, N.Y. 10022. Published simultaneously in Canada by Fitzhenry & Whiteside Limited, Toronto.

FIRST EDITION

Designer: Sidney Feinberg

Library of Congress Cataloging-in-Publication Data

Schwartz, Lynne Sharon.
We are talking about homes.

1. Landlord and tenant—New York (N.Y.)
2. Columbia University. I. Title.
KFX2022.S39 1985 346.74704'34 85-42735
ISBN 0-06-015479-9 347.4706434

---

85 86 87 88 89 HC 10 9 8 7 6 5 4 3 2 1

Contents

Acknowledgments

My deepest thanks go to the friends and neighbors whose stories appear in the following pages. By so generously offering their time and their memories, they made it possible for this book to exist. Thanks also go to Kenneth Schaeffer and Leonard Lerner, the attorneys who painstakingly helped me unravel the complexities of legal procedures and housing issues in New York City. My editor, Ted Solotaroff, with his rare instinct for form and narrative, had the vision to see the shape the material should take; and once again he gave me, with a durable grace, the best gifts an editor can extend to a writer—patience and trust. I am grateful above all to my husband, Harry Schwartz, who educated me from his enormous knowledge of and experience in urban planning and community activism, who went over the manuscript repeatedly with his usual scrupulous care and calm, and who unfailingly encouraged my efforts.

I also wish to thank the John Simon Guggenheim Memorial Foundation for its generous help and support during the writing of *We Are Talking About Homes.*

WE ARE TALKING ABOUT HOMES

1 Your House Is on Fire

Eighty-year-old Diana Angel Stamoulis remembers that there were Greek men working on the roof of her Manhattan apartment building on March 2, 1983. At about eleven in the morning, they banged on her door to tell her, speaking in Greek, that they saw smoke. "Stop making fun," she said, and closed her door. They banged again. This time she went out into the hall and opened the window. She saw smoke coming up from the fourth floor below. She climbed the stairs to the sixth floor, where she saw smoke coming from under the door of apartment 6D.

Mrs. Angel phoned her daughter Adrienne, an actress who lived in the building next door, and told her there was a fire. Adrienne also didn't believe it at first, but a short time later she arrived and the two women left the building, walking down the five flights of stairs. Once outside, where fire engines were already gathering in front of 547 Riverside Drive, Mrs. Angel decided to go back to save some of her possessions. There were thousands of dollars' worth of stamp collections, knickknacks, jewelry, a trunk full of fabrics—she had been a dressmaker like her mother before her—as well as valuable papers and correspondence with Mayor John Lindsay, Governor Nelson Rockefeller, and President Lyndon Johnson. Apparently no one saw her re-enter the building and climb the five flights.

In her seven-room apartment again, Mrs. Angel felt intense heat coming from 5D, next door. She heard the loud crashing of windows exploding from the heat, and when she looked out her kitchen window she saw flames. She sat down on her living room sofa and spoke to God in Greek. She said, "You're not going to let this building burn. But if it's time for me to go, I'll go with this building." At that moment the large mirror behind her, above the sofa, crashed and splintered, the glass flying right over her without hurting her. Mrs. Angel knew then that God felt it wasn't time for her to go.

Hot water coming from the ceiling fell on her left shoulder. She thought the building's boiler must have burst, and wondered how water from the boiler in the basement could have gotten so high up. She soon realized it was water that had been hosed into the floor above and heated by the flames. Mrs. Angel walked to her front window, facing Riverside Park and the Hudson River, thinking the falling water couldn't reach her there. Up on the hill across from the building, a small crowd of people who had gathered to watch the fire noticed her and waved at her to come down, but she shook her head. She was not afraid. She was "in a sort of trance," watching the beauty and the colors of the flames, hearing the loud crashing of windows. She stayed there, listening, and gazing at the gorgeous black and gray smoke, at the reds and blues and greens. "People don't realize how beautiful fire is."

For thirty-one years, Rebecca Rikleen had lived in this six-story building, owned by Columbia University, in the Morningside Heights section of Manhattan. She was visiting her youngest son's school, Hunter High, when she was notified about the fire through a series of telephone messages. A neighbor had called The Red Balloon, the day care center which Rebecca directs and which is located in another Columbia building, one block north of 547. Rebecca was not too disturbed by the news; many times there had been fires in the building or on the block—pork chop fires, she calls them—and firemen had put them out with no serious results. Still, she thought she'd better hurry over. "The taxi was halfway across the city and I could see rolls of smoke, a stream of smoke rolling towards the East Side. I couldn't imagine anything very bad. But the columns of smoke . . . As we were approaching, it was impossible to get near the building—there were twenty fire trucks on the block. I got out two blocks away and ran. You could see flames eating away at the building and leaping way up."

On the street, she met Chris, her daughter-in-law, who, with Rebecca's son Daniel and their two children, was staying with her temporarily. Chris had left a parrot and cats in the building and she was worried about them.

"We just stood there like idiots, waiting, not understanding or able to do anything about what we were seeing. Everyone was very frightened. There was excitement, the disrupted traffic, huge flames stories high, water streaming into the fire like it was nothing, like spitting on a fire to put it out. We were told to get out of the way, so we went up and watched from the hill on the upper level of the Drive, talking to each other in dumb ways, congratulating ourselves that we were there. The whole of the hill was full, impassable. The street was lined with fire trucks, double-parked. There was a truck for treating firemen, a truck for supplies, there were trucks backing out to refill the hoses."

Inge Irving, a travel agent and former actress who had lived in the building since 1957, was in her midtown office on March 2 when her son Jonathan called and said, "Mom, your house is on fire." "Yeah, thanks," she replied. "What else is new?" He told her he could smell the smoke from his own apartment, around the corner on Claremont Avenue. But Inge was too busy to leave her office—clients would be coming in all day, preparing for summer trips, and one employee was already out sick.

Both of Inge's sons watched the fire, Jonathan from the north corner at Tiemann Place, Victor from International House at the south end of the block, and both phoned her at intervals to report its progress. Meanwhile, Inge tried to get in touch with other tenants, some of whom were friends of long standing. She called the Silversteins, from 6D, who were vacationing in Florida—Inge had arranged their hotel reservation—but found they had just checked out. She was afraid of upsetting Selma Silverstein's elderly mother by phoning to ask where they had gone next. By the time Inge thought of a pretext to satisfy Selma's mother, another friend had already reached them. She called Nena O'Neill, a writer and anthropologist who lived in 6B, at her office downtown and left a message on the machine: "It's finally happened at last, Nena, just what we expected. The building's burning."

A tenant who had lived in 547 Riverside Drive for over twenty years was working in her apartment on the morning of March 2 when she heard the Greek workmen shouting in the hall and smelled smoke. She ran upstairs to the Silversteins' apartment to save their cat, which she was caring for while they were in Florida, and which she had fed only a few hours earlier. But their apartment was filled with smoke, and the workmen pulled her out before she could find the cat. While she was on the sixth floor she saw Mrs. Angel standing in the hall, very still, her eyes wide. "There's a fire, you have to get out, you have to get dressed," she told her, but Mrs. Angel didn't move.

Outside, a number of other tenants stood watching from the northern corner of the block, along with Anna Flanagan, the superintendent of the building; John Chandler, Columbia University's area manager; Nena O'Neill, who had found Inge's message, along with eight similar ones, on her machine; Jonathan Irving, who had grown up in the building but now lived around the corner; and a crowd of neighbors. Red Cross trucks gave out coffee and doughnuts, while the block was cordoned off and firemen herded people aside so that they could knock the glass from broken windows.

Joan Regelin, a singer, had lived in 547 Riverside Drive since 1965, when she was a graduate student at the Manhattan School of Music. In 1971 she married Christian Regelin, and the two now had three children, aged ten, eight, and six. Joan was coming home from a rehearsal in the late afternoon. "I'll never forget this image. It was a beautiful day, bright, windy, clear. I got off the bus—I usually take my car, but I didn't that day. I looked down the hill and realized the street was filled with fire trucks. And gradually, as I came closer and closer, I realized, That's my building. The first thing that came to my mind was, Where are the kids?

"There was a crowd of people standing around. The first person who came up to me was James Kyrimes, from the Columbia Housing Office. He stared at me with very clear, cold eyes, put his hand on my shoulder, and said, 'Your children are all right.' Someone else said, 'They're with your brother.' I was confused—my brother doesn't live in New York. I finally figured out my uncle had gotten the kids and taken them up to where he lives in Pelham.

"The next realization was that my car was sitting right in front of the building, covered with fire hoses and fragments of broken glass. I was just, I would say, in a state of shock. But something told me to move the car. The block was barricaded, but there were spaces further down the hill." Joan's concern for her car, as well as her ability to repark it on a narrow, hilly, two-way street lined with twenty fire engines, would not surprise anyone in 547. Over the years, Joan, tugging children, parcels, and paraphernalia in and out, was a familiar sight, whipping the neatest U-turns and maneuvering the car in and out of dazzlingly tiny parking spaces. Even more impressive, no matter what lavish civic and social events were taking place down the street at International House, what stately weddings or funerals of the august departed at The Riverside Church two blocks south, the Regelins' car managed to find a space right near the building, which made it the envy of every car owner in 547.

When the fire broke out, Coula Lurier, Diana Angel's younger sister, who lived in 1B, was at her senior citizens center. She had recently returned from her daughter's home in Washington, D.C., where she was recuperating from a series of radiation treatments. "Just in time for the fire," her son Harold later commented. Harold Lurier, a dapper, white-haired professor of medieval history at New York's Pace University, is the only man left from the original Dalianis family that came from Greece in 1904. He had rented the seven-room apartment in 1957, then moved into his own place farther uptown a year later, while his mother remained.

"My cousin Adrienne called me," he recalls, "and said, 'Sit down, the building's burning.' I went over and there it was, water was pouring in. My mother came and we ran into the house. There were no lights. We grabbed what we could and out we were. My mother went to Adrienne's apartment next door. I went in and out about three times, taking the TV, some silver, some jewelry. Did my Aunt Dina tell you how she could have died in the fire? No? She went back up after she had been persuaded to come out. She went into a closet, looking for a coat, and something fell against the closet door, jamming it and shutting her in. It just happened that James Kyrimes, from Columbia's Housing Office, was looking through the building and heard her calling. Otherwise she would have been killed there. Maybe she forgot."

As Mrs. Angel remembers it, a fireman noticed her standing at the front window looking out at the beauty of the flames. Very soon two firemen, along with Adrienne, came up the steps to get her. Mrs. Angel didn't want to go, but Adrienne took her by the hand and said, "Mother, these are only *things.* I need you." Together they led her out of the building. About a half hour later the roof of the apartment above collapsed and fell through to Mrs. Angel's apartment.

2 Being There

In 1964 we returned from a year in Rome, where Harry had a Fulbright grant to study urban history and planning. We had no money, no jobs, no place to live, and I was pregnant. We camped at my parents' house in Rockland County, and Harry would go into the city every day to look for an apartment. One day he came back pleased: six rooms in a nice old building on Riverside Drive, near Columbia, where we had both been students. I went with him to have a look. I saw mostly that it was big, and that its wide front windows overlooked the green of Riverside Park and the Hudson River. Soon after, Harry got a job at the New York City Planning Commission. It wouldn't make any sense for me to get a job, we agreed, since I would be having the baby in November, and it was almost September.

The day we officially moved in I took a good look around. The ceilings were very high, the walls all brown, and in the long hall, especially, they pressed in with a feeling of hushed desolation. I felt suddenly desolate too, and I cried. We began painting; my family came to help. My brother and my nephews painted the hall; my brother, who is very tall, could paint all the way up to the ceiling, past the molding, without a ladder. As he moved smoothly along the hall with his roller, turning it from brown to white, I stopped crying. It would be a place to live, for a while at least. We were nomadic. Before Rome we had lived in one apartment in New York, three in Philadelphia, and two in Boston, in the space of six years, so I expected we would keep moving. Because I was quite pregnant, I painted that segment of wall which could be reached without much bending or stretching. Every day I left a border on top for Harry to finish when he came home from work. Sometimes I would sit on the floor and creep around the perimeter of a room to do the lower moldings.

Among his many endeavors, my father, by profession a tax lawyer and CPA, had a furniture store in Chinatown. Since we had no furniture, it seemed natural to him that we should go to the store and pick out what we needed. Others like us, young people brought up in provincial sections of Brooklyn, would buy furniture when they set up house: bedroom suites, living room suites, and carpeting to match. But we wanted never to "set up house." We wanted to be the opposite of the way our families were, and to play house. Wherever we went, we made bookcases out of shelves and bricks and had big pillows in the living room. Our bed was a mattress on a frame. To placate my parents we did go to the store and pick out a few things—a round white kitchen table and four red chairs, a kitchen cabinet, and a couple of simple lamps. I remember my father looking with some contempt at one simple red lamp and saying, "That's all you want?" What we lacked in furniture we made up for on the walls—countless posters, prints, and odd hangings; over the years to follow we added works of art done by our children and some real works of art loaned by friends who were painters. Harry also cultivated eighty-two plants, so the place was green and not desolate.

Towards the end of the pregnancy I would sit at night in a red and white flowered wing chair we had gotten at some thrift shop and look out over the river at the bright lights of Palisades Amusement Park over on the New Jersey shore. I could see the outline of the roller coaster, all its snaking figure eights, and the cars swooping around them. I watched the moving letters on the park's huge marquee, advertising products I no longer remember, till I had memorized all the slogans in a trance of lethargy and muted panic over having a baby. The baby was late. Thanksgiving came and I called my mother to say I hadn't the strength to come to Rockland County for her big dinner. She had a solution. Hours later my mother and father and brother, my sister and brother-in-law and their two sons, marched in carrying the Thanksgiving dinner and set it up on paper plates, the first of many parties in our apartment. When they left I sat in the dark and watched the lights of Palisades Park, wondering when I would ever have this baby.

When Rachel was a few months old my mother began coming over once a week to stay with her so I could, in her words, "get out of the house." Soon I hired a woman from around the corner to come in one and a half days a week so I could get out some more. I found a part-time job writing publicity material for an open housing program in Harlem, which was close enough to walk to, and my mother remarked, "I always thought a woman should stay home with a baby, but in your case I see you can't. Go."

During six years of marriage, I had gone to work, and we had done the housework infrequently and together. Suddenly I found myself in a spacious, solid apartment with a baby it was universally assumed I should take care of, and wondered how on earth it had come about. I suppose both my parents were relieved I had married at all, since I had always threatened to do bizarre things with my life, and relieved that I had gone so far as to have a baby and do the conventional things for it like buy a crib and a playpen, dress it and feed it and take it to the park in a carriage with a hood and a row of plastic balls strung across the front. My mother told me things I ought to do for the baby; one was to give her a lamb chop for lunch when she got old enough to hold a bone. My mother believed in lamb chops the way later on people came to believe in yogurt and, more recently, in tofu. And once a week she arrived at around nine-thirty in the morning (my father dropped her off on his way to work) and I would fly out of the house to my job in Harlem.

When we took the apartment, the real-estate agent told us another couple just back from Rome had moved in on the third floor, both artists. Coming out of the elevator one day, I saw a young man who looked like he might be an artist, and who looked as new to the place as I did. I inquired and he said yes, he was the one, Bob Birmelin. We invited him and his wife, Blair, over for coffee. I tried to heat a frozen Sara Lee banana cake in the oven and ruined it—the frosting melted and dripped and I was embarrassed serving it. Nevertheless we became very good friends, especially Blair and I. I discovered she read Proust and Henry James and liked to sit and talk about books just as I did. Amidst our marathon talks, periodically there would be a new baby. First I had a girl, and a year and a half later she had a boy. I visited her in the hospital, bringing books, and when she came home with her baby we talked about childbirth and about the books. Two years later I had another girl, and a year and a half later Blair had another boy. We went to the park together, Riverside Park across the street, and in the course of an afternoon shifted our equipment from the benches near the slide to the benches near the jungle gym to the benches near the sandbox, along with other local mothers, women whose husbands were studying at Columbia or at Union Theological Seminary or Jewish Theological Seminary. I have a photo of Blair and me in heavy wool sweaters and jeans, playing hopscotch in the park. We look intent and defiant, as the children stand by and watch.

In our early years the park had a sprinkler for hot days, but one year it disappeared. Too much vandalism, the park man said. And the kids took water into the sandbox. I never understood what was wrong with taking water into the sandbox, but the park man, a jovial short dark man who liked to flirt with the mothers, was adamantly against it. He would sit and talk to any women alone, as if part of his job for the Parks Department was to keep young mothers company, and it was in fact pleasant to be flirted with at a time when babies and sandboxes constituted so much of the once variegated world. When he hurt his leg and disappeared soon after the sprinkler, I missed him equally.

After the park, Blair and I would take the children back to one of our apartments and have drinks while they played and fought. We would be talking about Proust or Henry James or the like, drinking and smoking, feeling like grown women, when one of the children would rush in insulted or injured, and we would have to mediate. I tried to settle disputes by reason and fairness, but in her house, I remember, she always gave the children apples. Blair seemed to have an unlimited supply of McIntosh apples, which seemed to soothe all injuries better than sweet reason. The children, especially as they all got older, made so much noise that it was a wonder we could manage to talk about Proust and James and such, but manage we did, and like my mother she helped rescue me; perhaps I did the same for her.

At night the four of us grownups would get together to eat and drink and play games like pick-up-sticks; it seemed all right to leave the children alone on the sixth floor or on the third, and dash out from time to time to check on them. We were all very competitive, and so the games of pick-up-sticks were tense. Especially we women were competitive, for the men were out working at their chosen professions while we had little outlet for our competitiveness. Probably we would have been competitive in any case. On and off we played with a Ouija board, which predicted the date of the birth of Blair's and Bob's first baby, the results of the 1968 presidential election, and later on spelled out the name of Rachel's nursery school teacher.

After a few years of babies and, for me, graduate school, we began to write fiction, Blair downstairs and I upstairs. She started first, after her second child was born. She had always been the painter and I the writer, at least in my mind. But there she was, writing. If a painter could write, I thought, surely I, a writer, could write too. When I had no private place to work she let me use a room in her apartment, so that sometimes we were both writing there, in different rooms. Now what we were both writing is in books and in bookstores, which seems miraculous.

Meanwhile, once a week for maybe seven years, my mother kept coming over to take care of the children while I got out. When I returned home I would find she had done some laundry and ironing too. She bathed the first baby, but with the second she said she couldn't anymore—she was older and this baby was heavier; her arm ached. But she took both out to the park, for she believed in fresh air as in lamb chops, and sometimes on her return she would rest for a few moments in the lobby on one of the old high-backed velvet-cushioned chairs that flanked a large oak breakfront. One day these pieces of furniture vanished. Stolen, our building superintendent, Mrs. Flanagan, said in amazement. The mystery of how and when these massive items could have been stolen was never solved. After that there was no furniture in the lobby.

My father would come by after work to pick my mother up, and we would sit and talk for a while, my mother enumerating what wondrous things the baby, and then babies, had done and said that day. During one of these talks the lights suddenly went out. First we thought it was our building alone, but out the window, up and down our side of the river as far as we could see, was blackness. Across the river New Jersey's lights were bright. We sat in the dark bemused. I unearthed a few candles. A neighbor from across the hall rang the bell to offer us a huge Christmas candle, and she sat with us for a while. She said she kept a lot of candles around for emergencies. She had the reputation of being eccentric, and indeed she had a touch of the Ancient Mariner about her, stopping us in the hall occasionally when some far-fetched topic seemed to weigh on her mind. She didn't have a glittering eye, but she did have a pale, waxy-looking face, as if she never went outdoors, and her hair was done in two long braids wound about her head like an Edwardian heroine's. She wore strange dun-colored shabby clothes that also seemed never to have seen the light of day—there was an overall mustiness to her—and those who had been in the building longer than we had told fantastic tales about primeval chaos in her apartment; and she had some strange habits as well, like reading late at night on the hall steps, to save electricity, she explained when we jumped back, startled, at the elevator door. She was often seen carrying shopping bags in and out, and she drove a repainted mail truck, which took up more than its share of precious street parking space. But with all that she could be pleasant to talk to, and she was intelligent. She was a public school teacher. And so we sat there bemused by the blackout—none of us could remember this happening in New York City before.

Soon my parents groped their way down the stairs. When they got home my mother called to describe to me how strange New York had looked from across the river, black and empty like an abandoned city. All evening, people in our building roamed the stairs and halls with flashlights, seeing if everyone was all right, if everyone had candles. It felt like a great adventure. But later on I was frightened, alone in the dark with a year-old baby. Even when the lights were on I was often afraid that something terrible would befall the baby and that I would not know the right thing to do. How much worse in the dark. It must have been from my mother that I had the notion that for every eventuality—particularly in the case of children—there was a right thing to do, as opposed to any number of wrong things, and that the acquiring of wisdom was learning all those right things in advance. Harry got home around midnight. He had walked all the way from the Lower East Side in stages, stopping off at friends' houses along the way, resting and gathering strength in the various darknesses. He brought news of the outside, like a courier in the Dark Ages.

Around this time Harry's family—mother, sister, cousins, and all—decided to have a surprise party for Harry's father's seventieth birthday in our apartment. Well, fine, except we hardly had suitable furniture. We felt we should dignify the occasion with a couch, at the very least. We did have a couch of sorts, but it was ragged and falling apart, having traveled to Philadelphia and to Boston and languished in storage for a year. Harry went to an auction in Brooklyn on the day of the party and found an elegant, old-fashioned tufted couch for eleven dollars, plus twenty-five to have it delivered the same day. The couch was white, which I thought beautiful. I was very proud of it when all the family arrived. Later my mother informed me that, beautiful or not, the white was merely the muslin that belonged under a covering. I didn't doubt this; she knew all about such things. She said we ought to have it covered. "Slipcovers," like "bedroom suite" and "carpeting," was a word connoting things Harry and I did not want any connection with. We kept it white for a long time. At last—perhaps our principles began to lapse or perhaps it was simply the dirt—we had it covered (though not with slipcovers) in blue velvet, which, even with my father's upholstery liaisons, cost many times more than the couch itself and the delivery. Blue velvet was beautiful too; that became the couch our children and our friends' boys from downstairs jumped on and off for many years. It was destroyed in the fire. Not burned: the living room window frame collapsed on it, doing more damage in one instant than four children over twelve years.

The feeling of having one's things desecrated was not new to us, though. Twice, while the babies were small, I came home to find the apartment had been burglarized. Drawers emptied onto the floor, a typewriter my father had given me when I was in high school gone, a watch, cufflinks, jars of pennies, gone. Both times I rang our next-door neighbors' bell and they came over to commiserate. George and Nena O'Neill, with their sons Michael and Brian, had moved in the same week we did, and we had become friendly comparing notes about painting those fine high-ceilinged rooms with their interminable moldings. George said if I was ever home alone and burglarized, I must bang on his door and he would come with his machete. As anthropologists, he and Nena had traversed jungles in Mexico and South America, and besides the machete had brought back Latin American rugs, wall hangings, and masks that decorated their apartment. Late one afternoon as I was stirring sweet and sour chicken in an electric frying pan, I heard footsteps in the hall. Harry was at work, Rachel with a friend down the street, and Miranda in her crib. The sweet and sour chicken was for a Barnard College freshman for whom I was a Big Sister, and her visiting parents from Cleveland. I advanced into the hall armed with my vegetable spoon and saw a skinny boy in a porkpie hat coming towards me. My face froze, a prefiguring, for I recognized my end. We both stopped moving at the same time, as in *High Noon.* After an eon I asked what he wanted, though I thought I knew. I was wearing a striped minidress. Too much of me was exposed, I felt; certainly he would want to rape me and then possibly kill me. He said he came to tell me the house was on fire and the hall was full of smoke. I walked past him to open the door and see. The hall was not full of smoke—he had climbed through a bedroom window. He walked past me and out, turned back to jeer, then went up the steps to the roof. I banged on George's door. Wearing a bathrobe, he ran for his machete and chased the boy. Buddy Maggart, an actor who lived on the fifth floor, joined in, but they never caught him. The police arrived to do their everlasting paperwork, and I finished cooking the chicken—it seemed pointless not to—and everyone came and ate it. For a year I was nervous about being in the apartment alone, then it passed.

The O'Neills' best-selling book on contemporary mores, *Open Marriage,* was reviewed in *The Village Voice* in 1972 by a critic who fantasized about the authors' holding group orgies on Mexican rugs with their next-door neighbors. We all had a laugh over this, since all we ever did with the O'Neills was talk lengthily in the hall, and visit now and then for drinks; also we went to their Christmas parties and George came gallantly to my aid with his machete. We were both couples who argued a lot, in loud voices, near our front doors. We never took each other's arguments very seriously, but we were well aware, tacitly, of their styles and contents, and that knowledge established an intimacy very different from the kind that would have existed had we had group orgies on Mexican rugs. The uncanny thing about the *Voice* reviewer's fantasy was that the O'Neills did in fact have Mexican rugs.

For sixteen years we watched their sons and they watched our daughters grow up. I admired Nena's elegance. She had left Akron, Ohio, years earlier to attend Barnard College and loved New York so much that she stayed. She became one of those warmly earthy kinds of women who manage to look glamorous even when their spirits are frazzled: dark hair streaked with gray, olive complexion, and soft, pensive features, tinted glasses and flowing, colorful clothes. She had a distinctively low voice which seldom veered from its mellow composure. A reasonable, tolerant, yet dashing middle-aged woman—everything I had no hopes then of ever becoming. Assiduous, too. Early one morning, when I opened the door to investigate the rapid rhythmic sounds coming from the hall, I found her jumping rope. She seemed faintly abashed to be discovered, but kept on jumping. After that, whenever I heard the morning sound of her rope slapping against the linoleum, I felt the sense of security that rituals—even those of other people—afford.

Then one September evening I met Nena coming into the lobby. I hadn't seen her all summer and so we fell into each other's arms. She started to cry and said George was dying. He had septicemia and was in St. Vincent's Hospital in Greenwich Village. I tried to encourage her, but people are usually right about such things, and George died in October of 1980. At the funeral, Jerry Silverstein, an actor and broadcaster who lived just across the hall, spoke long and eloquently about his friendship with George, their late-night talks, their seeing each other through hard times. Jerry and his wife, Selma, had been closer to the O'Neills than we had—though neither had they had orgies on the Mexican rugs. Only long friendship.

This was not our first loss. Bob Hedges on the second floor, widowed, genial, lonely, always helping out in the community, had died. Many of us attended a memorial service in The Riverside Church up the street. Bob's children (once our baby-sitters), grown now but still recognizable, returned from their homes out of town to sit with the neighbors in the church. Rebecca Rikleen's husband, Alexander, an architect, had died, leaving her with four children: Sander, the oldest son, in law school, Daniel and Annie in college, and Ethan, who was then seven. Rebecca, a tall woman with a mane of long brown hair and an air of competence, had been in the building almost longer than anyone—since 1951, when she moved into a first-floor apartment with her parents and two younger brothers. After Rebecca married, her parents and brothers moved elsewhere, leaving the couple the apartment, where they remained and raised the four children.

Ben Irving, an assistant executive secretary of Actors Equity and unofficial mayor of our building, had also died. Ben used to take care of everyone's problems, large and small. Particularly if you were having trouble with the landlord, you called Ben. He was universally available and loved for his warmth and wit and generous spirit—a big robust man with a ruddy face, a booming voice, and thinning honey-colored hair. Jerry Silverstein, who had gone to college with Ben in the 1940s and known his first wife, who died leaving two small children, said he had always been that way. Ben moved into 547 in 1956 with Debby and Jonathan, and in 1957 Inge, an actress, moved in with him. They were married the following year, and Victor was born in 1960. For a while Inge continued to work in the theater, but finally going to auditions became too difficult with three young children, and she became a travel agent, together with her sister, Eva.

Inge and Ben used to give large parties, stretching over afternoons into the late evenings, where food overflowed and neighbors and friends, many of them theater people, drifted in and out with children of all ages. And then one day in 1968, when the Irvings were returning from a vacation, Ben had a heart attack in the lobby of 547. Inge called for help and did mouth-to-mouth resuscitation until the ambulance from St. Luke's Hospital arrived, too late. He was forty-eight. At his funeral, so crowded that people had to stand at the back, the actor and folk singer Theodore Bikel said the Kaddish. Bikel said that though Ben may not have wanted a religious service, he himself wanted Kaddish said for his friend and so he was going to say it. The poet Eve Merriam, a next-door neighbor and friend of the family, wrote and recited a memorial poem which began:

> In a world where friend and neighbor
> are old-fashioned words,
> he was an old-fashioned man.
>
> In a world where honor and kindness
> have not yet found a place,
> he was a man of the future. . . .
>
> All who knew him claim kinship. . . .

I went down to Inge's the morning after Ben died to offer to buy some groceries. She was sitting in a chair looking weak, surrounded by family, not only her three children but her sister Eva and Ben's sister Esther. Inge was always a forceful, highly assertive person—it was unsettling to see her weakened. Assertive she still was: she said I could not only get the groceries—Esther would give me a list—but also over the weekend perhaps Harry and I could take Victor out somewhere for a change of scene. In the evening Harry and I went down to visit. Jonathan, who was thirteen and always a wise child, said that if it had to be, it was better that it was his father who died—he couldn't have borne losing another mother. Over the weekend we took Victor, who was seven, on a boat ride to the Statue of Liberty, along with Rachel. It started to rain on the ferry, a chill, stinging rain; Rachel cried and we had to take turns carrying her; I was pregnant again and the climb up to the torch was arduous. Later I thought we might have come up with something better. To this day I sometimes think, why, of all places, the Statue of Liberty, which Harry and I had seen before and Rachel was too young to appreciate and Victor, in his state of grief, probably didn't care about?

A year or so after the Statue of Liberty, Rachel began attending a free nursery school run by the Parks Department in Morningside Park, ten blocks away. Lots of kids from the neighborhood went. On Riverside Drive, Tiemann Place, and Claremont Avenue flourished the oldest established permanent floating cooperative walking pool: each parent made only two trips a week but they were epic—half a mile with six four-year-olds. I took Rachel and Julienne Maggart from the fifth floor, and pushed Miranda in a stroller. Picking up the third and fourth kids was tolerable, but the fifth and sixth stops were harrowing, what with heavy front doors, timed buzzers, stairs, stroller, elevators, traffic, and the nature of children. There existed two imperfect strategies for getting the children safely across wide and heavily traveled Broadway and Amsterdam Avenue—in one mighty swoop or in shifts. I chose the swoop, never daring to let them get behind me. One of the mothers, an experienced one with four children, took a shortcut on snowy days through Cherry Park up on the Drive. Its attraction was an enormous flight of stone steps completely obliterated by snow. She let the kids slide down one by one, then slid down herself.

Julienne's father, Brandon, or Buddy, as we called him then, did the nursery school trek with the nonchalance of a father of five, and at first my children, each in turn, were thrilled since they saw him daily in the Buddy and Jim comedy skit on *Sesame Street.* Also, any time Buddy appeared in a television commercial—touting the softness of a baby's diaper or twirling pizza dough—they would call us to come and watch. But very quickly they grasped that Buddy, however nonchalant, made them hold hands like the rest of us, and not run in the street, and the experience became far less thrilling. Soon they would even stop calling us to the TV screen but lackadaisically, hours later, let fall the news that Buddy was now doing wine or chocolate.

Accidental gatherings in the halls, the lobby, or at the elevator door propelled the life of the building like the conjunctions that take place at nerve endings. With the Silversteins, we held long and rather grandiose conversations at the elevator door, all about our lives and aspirations. The Silversteins were two of the most energetic and bouncy people I had ever met. They were always jogging or playing tennis, and would turn up at the elevator in their various sporting costumes, with their reverberating actors' voices and beaming faces, and sometimes they would scold me because, with my babies trailing after me and my vague dreams of being a writer in abeyance, I wasn't lively enough for their high standards of *joie de vivre.* They were a wonderfully matched pair, Jerry dark and earnest and cheerful, Selma fair and wry and practical—even their squabbles were entertaining, like a performance. They had married way back in 1947 and spent their early summers acting in summer theater. During those years Jerry worked as a teacher, while Selma acted: she was in the Greenwich Village Circle in the Square's first production, *Dark of the Moon,* in *A Majority of One* on Broadway, and in many off-Broadway plays and radio and TV commercials.

But at the time I knew them, Selma was already bouncing on to something new; she was studying for a master's degree in social work and planned to become a therapist, and naturally she recommended therapy for everyone, in her energetic, wry way. And Jerry was now on TV every week, doing a news program for children, which won countless awards; at the elevator he would stop to tell me the topic of the week—the death of Nasser, or New York City's water shortage. If I had time I would watch and marvel at the way he conducted panel discussions with kids, inquiring into their opinions with the greatest respect and attention. And always, at the elevator, one of us would finally say, How silly to stand here at the door, let's get together for an evening. The evening would arrive: We would eat and drink; Jerry would tell jokes with Yiddish punch lines that he translated for Harry, and Selma would tell anecdotes about Jerry's large and forthright family, especially his brother the rabbi, whose pithy pronouncements she rendered so vividly that when I finally met him at one of the Silversteins' family Chanukah parties I felt I already knew him. And so these evenings would laugh themselves by, with little said about our grander aspirations. Soon we would meet at the elevator again. . . .

The Silversteins' son Kenny was our baby-sitter, and the O'-Neills' son Brian, and Inge's three children, Debby, Jonathan, and Victor in turn, and Rebecca Rikleen's daughter Annie from the third floor, and Yvonne Uehling from the first floor. To this day, our children can rate them all, now in their twenties and thirties, on the various aspects of baby-sitting. We know which ones slept on the job and which foraged for food and which talked on the phone all evening, as well as their varying degrees of patience and imagination. Jonathan Irving was a favorite because he would let the kids stand on his big shoes, facing him and gripping his hands, then walk them around with giant steps; this they found irresistible. Jonathan wrote a story for Rachel about the adventures of an umbrella, and bound it and presented it to her with a flourish; she still has it. Years later Rachel baby-sat for Joan Regelin's three children, on the second floor, and doubtless they can rate her too.

Joan was my unemployment companion. When New York City underwent its fiscal collapse in 1975, I lost my job teaching English at Hunter College, and would take the subway to Washington Heights every Monday to claim unemployment insurance. I stood in line in an enormous dingy green room that made everyone in it look dingy. There were about twelve lines stretching the length of the room, and about seventy or eighty people on each. Naturally I looked for the shortest line, but in the end it never made much difference. Joan, then a sporadically employed singer, sometimes collected unemployment at the same hour—three o'clock—and she offered to drive me up. She was a large, dark-haired, dramatic-looking woman perhaps around thirty then, with, like many singers, a rich, sensuous, persuasive speaking voice. While she zoomed a tortuous path up the West Side Highway, we had talks about our parents and our children. She told me about growing up the oldest in a family of five children in North Carolina. She told me, too, how her grandparents used to live on our block, three buildings down, in the building that was taken over by Union Theological Seminary and became a dormitory for married students—her grandmother was the last holdout tenant. And she told me some of the adventures and idiosyncrasies of her car, which she spoke of as a member of the family. The car, a plucky, mustard-colored 1971 Volvo which for many years had borne North Carolina plates, was something of a local legend, its adventures with crime and bureaucracy making it seem almost human. It had been stolen and retrieved, it had been towed away, it had weathered near-terminal illnesses. On weekends, Christian would often be in front of the house, washing it or applying first aid. (Little did we know then that in 1982 the car would suffer the ultimate indignity of being stolen for good.)

Joan took me to claim unemployment and I gave her outgrown toys and down jackets, and we sent the kids back and forth endlessly for cups of sugar and milk. After a year of standing in line I got my job back, and then the following year lost it again. But this time my unemployment depot was changed to Fifty-fourth Street. I missed the rides with Joan, not least the skill and verve of her driving, the energy with which she hauled that stick shift through its paces.

There were no longer as many children around when Joan's three were small. Columbia had bought the building in 1966 and from then on rented mostly to graduate students and junior faculty. But in the early years our daughters were part of a troop, the Maggarts' five, Blair's and Bob's two boys downstairs, a girl named Carla on the first floor, and Yvonne's younger brother, Gregory. Traipsing about on Halloween, they could never comprehend how Mrs. Lurier on the first floor, who gave the best treats—individually wrapped packages of homemade cookies—could be the same Mrs. Lurier who the rest of the year yelled to scare them off when they played in the lobby or in the courtyard right under her window.

Mrs. Lurier's sister, Mrs. Angel, on the fifth floor, was reputed to be strange as well, since, as she let everyone know, she was writing to President Lyndon Johnson, among other leaders, about the disability case connected with a portion of ceiling having fallen on her arm in 1963, aggravating an injury sustained at work two years earlier and making it difficult for her to continue as a dressmaker. She would talk about the evils of bureaucracy to whoever would listen. But I liked her and shared her feelings about the evils of bureaucracy, and given my verbal and vociferous and large family of Russian Jewish immigrants, I saw nothing strange about people expressing themselves in forceful and extreme ways; indeed, it made me nostalgic for my childhood, when stately people like Mrs. Angel—aunts and uncles—sat around oilcloth-covered tables dotted with glasses of amber tea and shouted at each other warmly. I also liked her because she admired my children and said so whenever we met. Since I had long ago given up broiling lamb chops for lunch, her pronouncements were reassuring. And I liked the way she looked, big and squarishly built, a square unlined face, high cheekbones and clear eyes, dark brown hair close to auburn pulled away from her forehead to show a widow's peak and done in a knot. Stern and formidable, she used to walk erectly down Riverside Drive with the gait of one who has business abroad in the world. I often imagined her up on an outdoor podium, exhorting crowds to justice and righteousness, and in fact she once told me she might have gone into politics like her father, had she been a man, and thought she would have done well, but that now, after three turbulent marriages—one arranged when she was sixteen, one "the love of her life," and one to an excitable Greek naval officer—and a lifetime crowded with incident, it was too late.

As a matter of fact it was politics that brought her to this country. In 1904 her father, George Dalianis, ran for office in his home town of Amalias, population 26,000, and lost. "In America," she said, "when they lose they shake hands and make up, but in Greece they could shoot themselves." To help Mr. Dalianis get over the pain of losing, the family set off on a trip to America, leaving Diana, only three months old, with her grandmother, who, as it turned out, brought her up till she was nine. Then in 1912 the Turkish war started, and her parents, who were prospering in the restaurant business, decided to bring her to America. When she arrived in Worcester, Massachusetts, she discovered, along with her older brother Peter, three more children born since the move—Coula, Joan, and Charles.

And when she spoke of these things, alternately laughing and scowling, her voice would traverse the scales, penetrating the air. She might well have been addressing a group rather than just a woman less than half her age, wide-eyed—her narration had that sweep and force of one born for public oratory. But when she laughed she became suddenly girlish and I could see she must have been a beauty. Eventually I even found out what the correspondence with Lyndon Johnson was all about. Because Mrs. Johnson's private secretary was a girlhood friend of Diana's daughter Adrienne, the President had actually responded to the pleas about the disability claim as well as sent Diana New Year's and other greetings, plus a book containing the laws he drew up while in Congress, plus a flag.

One Sunday afternoon Diana got stuck in the elevator of 547. Getting stuck was not unusual; ours was a highly capricious elevator. Among its whims was a periodic refusal to sort out the numbers above 4. During those spells, if your destination was 5 you pressed 6, and if it was 6 you pressed 7, which was the roof. People who got stuck pushed the alarm button, setting loose a loud and terrible clanging which those of us on the top floor had learned to distinguish from the loud and terrible clanging set off when the roof door was illicitly opened. At the sound of the elevator alarm we would stream out in the halls to shout encouragement to the prisoner until Mrs. Flanagan or her brother, Tom Kelly, either fixed it or called the elevator men.

Diana Angel was not a patient victim; invisible, she shouted furiously about her nerves and her stress—everyone of course understood she had been tried to the limit by the ceiling falling. Finally Tom Kelly induced the elevator to come within a foot of our floor, and, even more difficult, induced Diana to climb out, shaken, trembling, and vociferous. She came to our apartment for a cup of tea. Calm at last, her stalwart self emergent, she pronounced as usual that my children were very well brought up.

Tom Kelly lived in the basement apartment with his sister, Anna Flanagan, and helped her out with chores in the building. I was put off by him at first because when he drank he was silent and sullen. He would answer the door looking irritated beyond measure and quickly get his sister to deal with the complaint. But when he wasn't drinking—and for long periods he would stop, till he stopped altogether—he was wry and witty, with a fund of mordant comments on life in its most grand or petty manifestations. During his dry spells he would often get jobs in other buildings around town as a doorman or elevator operator, and set off for work very well dressed and very brisk. But these jobs never lasted long.

From May to October, Tom and his sister, and the super from next door and her daughter, would sit out on the ledge in front of our building every evening, taking the air. We never had a doorman like more elegant buildings farther south: the party of supers, sharp-eyed and vigilant, was for a long time the closest we got to any sort of guardianship. Comings and goings provided the raw material for their criticism of life. Boyfriends and girlfriends of our teenagers were duly assessed, and reports to the parents submitted promptly, though unsought. Passing by, I would stop to catch up on local news delivered in Tom's trenchantly satirical style. He liked children and would tease mine, when they were small, asking them to take him along to school or to camp—perhaps he had fantasies of escape from the basement into a life of youthful capers—and at first they were leery because he was gruff, with a low, snarling voice that sounded like it had snaked its way through a wringer, besides which he had an ailment that made his head lean permanently to one side. But once they got past these traits they grew fond of him too. When Tom brought plumbers or plasterers to our apartment, he would hang around diverting me with his snarling opinions on everyone in the building, and also cadge cigarettes, since he had to have a cigarette dangling from his lips at all times. He was a thin, white-haired man with a caved-in chest and a squarish face: rheumy blue eyes, pinkish cheeks, full lips, and a dangling cigarette. While plumbers probed, we would discuss the atrocious state of the sixth-floor apartment across the hall, to which the tenant refused to give Mrs. Flanagan a key, and to which she admitted no repairmen. Yes, Tom would grunt bitterly, it was a terrible hazard.

Tom knew I was a writer; in the fall of 1981 he asked if I would write a letter for him to a CBS News commentator who had broadcast a segment about a chewing gum that supposedly helped people stop smoking. He snarled that it was only fair I should do this since I had rung his bell with a complaint while he was watching the TV news, and because of my interruption he hadn't caught the name of the gum. I wrote to CBS News a few times and finally telephoned. The name of the gum was Nicorette, I reported back to Tom, but it wasn't yet available in the United States, only in Europe. He accepted this news ruefully, his cigarette drooping. A few months later I was in Italy, where I'd promised him I'd look for the gum, but I didn't find it. Tom developed lung cancer and would go for what his sister called X-ray treatments. He was glum and resigned about his disease, and when we all tried to encourage him with visions of recovery, he would nod sarcastically and snarl. He grew weak. His chest caved in even more. He kept smoking. He said he might as well, now. Before I left for Iowa in the summer of 1982, where I had a temporary teaching job, he asked me to ring his bell and say hello when I came home for vacations, which I did. He never asked me in—that was not part of our friendship—but at the door he brought me up to date on which elderly neighbors were growing eccentric and exactly how, who was moving out to greener pastures, whose children were getting married or going away to school, and the observable love life of the recently divorced; also how his disease was progressing, and how hard it was to stop smoking. After the fire, Columbia moved Tom and his sister to a tiny apartment ten blocks south on 113th Street, which they hated. He died about a month later, in the spring of 1983. I was still away and was sorry I could not go to his funeral as a final tribute, but even more sorry that I never got to hear what he would have snarled about the fire. Soon after he died, the gum was approved for sale in the United States.

Our apartment had a big living room and dining room joined by an archway, both rooms facing west, graced by large windows overlooking the park and the river with its boats going by. We painted that windowed wall red, and it framed the outdoors. North, we could see all the way up to the George Washington Bridge. In spring and summer the trees in the park were so lushly leaved we could barely see the water through them, but in winter and fall the view was broad and clear. On windy days there were whitecaps all along the river so that it looked like a printed fabric billowing about, or the wet fur of a large beast with the shivers. Often in winter ice would clog it for weeks at a time, huge chunks of jagged ice like cold driftwood, and for those weeks no ships could pass. Sometimes a ship got stuck and stayed there for days at a time, till the ice melted. Most of the ships we saw were barges or small cargo ships or the Circle Line taking tourists on a pleasure cruise around Manhattan Island, but now and then a good-sized ship would float by, and when the children were small I would call them to watch. Even when they were older, I still sometimes called them for a truly spectacular ship.

Also out the living room windows, across in Riverside Park, was the big hill all the neighborhood kids and their parents used for sledding. Early on, Harry and I would go out sledding with the kids; in later years we could keep an eye on them from the window, as they skimmed down and trudged up, dragging the sleds behind them. But the finest things we watched from the window were the sunsets, especially the late ones, June through October. We abandoned cooking, eating, or homework to rush to the window, for once it began, each instant's configuration of clouds and color above the Palisades, of light and shadow on the surface of the water, could vanish in a trice. Irreverent, we even rated them—better than yesterday's, not so fine as last Sunday's —and sometimes on summer evenings we were lured out to walk along the Drive, to get closer up. We grew to be connoisseurs, knowing from the way each sinking began whether it would be drawn out or abrupt, magnificent or humble, whether it would start out splendid and dissipate, or start out nondescript and turn splendid, whether the best part would be just before or just after the sun went down. We could tell from the formations of the clouds and the color of the air, pink, or violet, or amber, and sometimes even a pale weird lime green.

Off the once-desolate long hall were three bedrooms, medium-sized, small, and very small. The advantage of the very small one was its own private bathroom—it must have been a maid's room in the days when the building housed the rich. Harry and I always had the small back bedroom as our own, but the other two rooms went through countless changes of role over nineteen years, mostly depending on the phases of our children. When they could live and sleep peaceably together we used the tiny room as a study, two desks crowded in. When they couldn't we moved elsewhere: in the end, I wrote three books under our loft bed. But way back in the sixties, I don't remember what I expected to do at a desk —I don't remember any plans except a vague notion that somehow I would become a writer, as if it happened to a person like puberty or gray hair. I did some translations in the medium-sized room during Rachel's first year, as well as a few free-lance proofreading and editing jobs. Eventually, in the seventies, I dropped out of graduate school to write, because being a writer showed no signs of happening to me like puberty or gray hair. In the tiny bedroom I wrote my first published article, a Watergate satire, in June of 1974. When it was published Harry made a big party with all our friends to celebrate: there was a feeling of buoyancy abroad over the climax of Watergate, with its satisfying cast of heroes and villains.

That party took its place in the annals of parties held in the apartment, parties like the snows of yesteryear. Sometimes now we recall and compare them—the New Year's Day party thrown together that morning, where Rachel at a mere twelve years old concocted a triumphant eggnog; and the surprise party for Harry's father which occasioned our getting the white couch; and then the party for Harry's fortieth birthday, when he got piles of presents like a child; and the July 4 party in the Bicentennial year, when friends gathered on our tarred roof to watch the glorious procession of tall-masted and bannered ships parade up the Hudson all that long sunny summer afternoon. Parties the children cannot remember, Halloween parties where guests masqueraded as their secret selves, a frog, a toad, Lolita and Superman and Al Capone. Not to mention the two children's birthday parties a year with the requisite balloons and whistles, parties I smiled through because I poured Scotch—which can pass for apple juice—into my paper cup.

Like a person, the apartment had a few chronic ailments. The bedroom doors never closed completely. The closet in the largest bedroom had no door. We never got around to asking the landlord for one, and hung up a curtain instead. The shower didn't drain properly—one stood ankle-deep in water. The plumbers who came to remedy this once and for all were a merry troop who stayed for days, creating chaos out of order, but in the end nothing much was changed. In the tiny bathroom in the erstwhile maid's room, a leak in the pipes in the wall would spring mysteriously every New Year's holiday. We had no evidence of it, but the Launays in 5A or Inge in 4A would call to report that water was pouring down from the ceiling. Eventually Inge had only to call on New Year's, say hello in a certain wry tone, and we would know. After a few years the plumbers didn't bother to plaster up the wall when they were finished, but simply put in a wooden panel that could be easily removed the following New Year's.

I knew every person in every one of those twenty-four apartments until the last few years, when Columbia began putting students in and the students, just passing through, were not interested in knowing their neighbors. But for most of the nineteen years I knew the feel of people's apartments, the furnishings and the quality of the light on the different floors, people's relatives—Jerry's brother the rabbi, Inge's sister Eva and Ben's sister Esther—and their children, what schools they went to and how they turned out. I watched as Yvonne Uehling, our babysitter, a slender, shy, soft-spoken girl, became a beauty at fifteen or sixteen; for a year or so we all endured crowds of boys mooning outside on the front step waiting for an appearance, a word, a glance. Together we also endured the summer Columbia replaced our ever-ailing boiler, when those of us with no vacation plans learned how to take cold showers, which is not so hard once you get used to it. Worse to endure was the collapse of the wall separating our back courtyard from the opposite building, on Claremont Avenue—a mighty and prolonged roar on a still Saturday afternoon. We were in the papers, notorious. For weeks our gigantic heap of rubble was a place of interest for the locals, less historically evocative than Riverside Church or Grant's Tomb, where tourists went, but more dramatic for those in the know. Apparently Columbia had been aware of the tremulous wall for some time, but had been haggling with the Claremont Avenue landlord over whose responsibility it was to fix it. At last workmen arrived with cement trucks and sacks of sand and gravel. They began their dragging and drilling at six in the morning, which incensed Buddy Maggart most of all since he worked nights and slept mornings. When the wall was rebuilt months later, Mrs. Flanagan and Tom complained bitterly, since the courtyard they had used to hang out wash and grow plants and cool off in on hot nights was a third of its original size.

I knew when Mrs. Flanagan's son had a heart attack and exactly how overweight he was. I could even remember the days when Mrs. Flanagan, a talkative kind of super, complained that her son and his wife had no children; then, overnight it seemed, there were four, and her talk switched to proud anecdotes of the grandchildren. When they visited she even brought them up to display them. I knew when Joan's son hurt his head and she feared there might be serious damage but there wasn't, and when Jerry Silverstein suffered from tennis elbow; and when Ethan Rikleen was hit by a car and stayed in Roosevelt Hospital for weeks with a leg injury. Likewise everyone knew when Rachel tumbled off the back of Yvonne's bike in the park and I rushed her, holding the torn ball of the bleeding finger in place with a towel, to the emergency room at St. Luke's Hospital in the back of a passing police car. Police don't like to take passengers, but they didn't refuse. Everyone knew that if you called an ambulance you'd go to Sydenham Hospital, farther away, and it was better all around to get to St. Luke's if you could. Everyone knew, too, when a man in the building next door was killed by a speeding car at the corner, and then finally the city put up the traffic light we had long been asking for, with a pedestrian button as a bonus.

I had been inside Grant's Tomb and climbed to the top of Riverside Church during the ringing of the carillon bells, and ridden my bike in Riverside Park; I knew who played tennis there and who ran, and who, like us, had picnics. Where people walked their dogs, who cleaned up after them and who didn't. Who walked around late at night and who was afraid to. Who was mugged, when and where and how. Mrs. Lurier of the Halloween cookies, beaten up in her apartment and no one heard her scream —an empty Saturday afternoon in spring. Inge, coming home from work, by a boy with a knife. Joan, bringing home groceries. Nena, on the subway steps. We organized a tenants' association on the block. Harry was the chairman. With money from those willing to pay, we hired a uniformed guard to patrol at night: genteel Mr. Crawford, who reported for duty in a shiny black Cadillac. The supers taking the air resented his presence, as if it impugned their ability to keep the street safe, but that did not stop them from including him in their nightly conferences on the ledge.

It was hardly possible to get down that street without stopping to talk. Over the years we came to know people all up and down the block, and when the old ones stopped appearing we knew they had died. I didn't like everyone equally, but it was scarcely a question of liking. They came with the territory, and when they moved or died I missed them. It is possible to miss even people you don't like.

I never liked the apartment that much either, or never thought I did. I found it cramped. Despite its six rooms there never seemed to be enough privacy, though perhaps it was the way we lived, with no clear boundaries and turfs, that inhibited privacy. And the neighborhood wasn't safe, especially at night, even during the years Mr. Crawford patrolled with his reassuring black Cadillac. I also never quite forgot the three dreadful spells when we had mice, and how Jonathan Irving of the big shoes came up and baited our traps with chocolate—he claimed mice preferred chocolate to cheese and judging from the results he was right. Yet now it strikes me that I lived in that apartment longer than any other place in my life, and the placement of the furniture and the pots and pans and the pictures on the walls seems fixed and preordained, the only way we could have lived.

There are times, opening my eyes in the morning, when I am astonished to find myself in alien surroundings; I close my eyes, not yet fully awake, and imagine taking my old route through the morning, first to the front windows to look out at the park and river and see what kind of day it might be. Only lately, more than a year after the fire, do I allow myself to remember in detail how it was to move through those rooms in patterns developed over the years; how, when it rained, I whisked from room to room in a well-worn path closing windows, then stood in the front watching it pour into the abundant river; how we put speakers in the kitchen so I could hear records while I cooked; how I was lulled to sleep watching old movies on TV up in the loft bed; and how, as I talked on the kitchen wall phone, my eyes panned every plane of the room, so every square foot is now forever printed on my retina—yellow walls, dark green cabinets, striped curtain, the arrangement of pots and pans on a dark red pegboard; the plastic magnetic letters on the refrigerator that our grown children still fooled with, messages like Happy Anniversary or Good Luck on SAT's, or messages from their friends—Julie Was Here; and the round white table which, to my father's gratification, we bought at his store, and the orange chairs. For after my father's red plastic chairs gave out we replaced them with wooden ones bought for a dollar each from a local synagogue that was clearing out old furniture. I made covers out of bright printed corduroy for their ugly plastic seats, covers that looked like shower caps, and the children, aware of my limitations in the domestic arts, laughed at them, but lo, when stretched out they fit perfectly.

I remember most of all being pregnant with my first baby in that apartment, and towards the end, when it was an effort even to move, sitting in the old wing chair looking out over the river, and watching the moving lights over Palisades Amusement Park advertising things I cannot remember now but which twenty years ago I knew by heart. I would watch the letters slide by again and again, wondering what it would be like to be a family in that apartment, wanting the pregnancy over but fearing the birth, and falling into a trance induced by the glitter of the faraway roller coaster. Maybe I might live in that static condition, pregnant forever, a permanent trance. Years later they tore down Palisades Amusement Park to replace it with two high-rise apartment buildings which were nothing at all to look at. But on clear nights we could still lean out the window and see the strand of lights that was the George Washington Bridge looping the water.

We were ignorant then, our lives full of vast and unformed possibilities that narrowed and congealed to specifics. In that apartment we raised two children, and I made myself into a writer instead of dreaming it, and I learned that the getting of wisdom is something other and more fruitful than finding out the right things to do on every occasion. By the end, the family forced out was four grown people, two of whom had never known any other home.

3 Some Correspondence

October 2, 1974*

Dear Evelyn,

It's been a week exactly since you went away leaving your radio on loudly enough to disturb many of the residents of this building. We heard it all evening and all night. . . . Many people . . . complained that this wasn't the first time that they'd been prevented from working or sleeping by your radio.

Early Thursday we phoned Mrs. Flanagan to turn the blasted thing off. . . . She came up here, knocked, heard the radio and was afraid to enter alone, in case you'd met with foul play. She asked some of us to stand by. When she opened the door, the little she could because of the assorted debris piled behind and around it, we were appalled. Your apartment is a filthy, cluttered mess. To call it a health and fire hazard is to understate it. Now we understand why foul smells have always permeated our end of the sixth floor hallway. . . .

Years ago, when Jerry helped your father when he was

*The letters in this chapter are only a brief selection; others along the same lines were lost in the fire.

ill, he first saw the shocking mess. At the time, Mr. Slain, the landlord's representative, had to break in to repair a leaky pipe; he rang our bell to ask us to bear witness to the unbelievably disgusting condition of the apartment then. After that, for a long time, a stream of people helped you cart out debris in large quantities at all hours of the night. We presumed that the improvement had lasted. We were wrong.

How you choose to live in your own house in the country is entirely your own business. In an apartment house, it's your neighbors' business. You expose us to the dangers of fire and vermin. We all owe it to each other to help maintain safe living conditions for all in this building. The condition of your apartment, the heaped up stuff, the piles of inflammable material, endanger our lives.

Many of your neighbors are very angry. They have drafted a strong letter of complaint to be sent to Columbia University. They have, however, decided to let us try this personal appeal first. Evelyn, you must never again disturb our rest by leaving your radio on late (or all) night; and—you must clean up the apartment.

We expect to hear from you about this within the next few days. Ring our bell before 11 P.M., phone or write us a note about your intentions.

Your neighbors,
Jerry and Selma Silverstein

In her prompt reply (written the same day), Evelyn (not her real name) promised to "tackle immediately what can fairly be called inflammable." She even offered to supply a weekly report, adding, "I'm not being sarcastic." A week later, in a note to a neighbor, she stated that she was cleaning every evening and throwing things out every morning. The next portion of the correspondence that survived was dated about two years later.

November 30, 1976

Dear Evelyn:

Again we've come to the point where we have to express our feelings as your immediate neighbors about the conditions in your apartment.

On Sunday, the 28th of November, Mrs. Flanagan had to enter your apartment to investigate the source of a leak. Water was dripping down into apartment 5C from a leaky radiator in your apartment, 6C. Again, Mrs. Flanagan found the same shockingly filthy, cluttered, roach-infested conditions that have alarmed all of us on previous occasions when an unexpected event forced someone to enter your apartment in your absence.

She was appalled at what she saw. Once the door was opened (that is, as far as the piled-up debris would permit), she was made dramatically aware once again of the danger your apartment poses for all of us: not only to those of us on the sixth floor but to every man, woman, and child in this building. . . .

Consider what would happen if a fire would break out. As you know, excessive clutter is an incendiary precondition to fire—faulty wiring, a spark, anything could explosively ignite and feed on this inflammable material. Fire in this over-sixty-year-old building would be catastrophic. Given your mountains of inflammable materials, there wouldn't be a chance for survival.

In the past there have been instances where the official city service departments and the Columbia management authorities have had to enter your apartment for various reasons. . . . At one time, prodded by the authorities, you did clean up somewhat. Now we are shocked to find that the same conditions that were intolerable in the past still continue to exist and, in fact, have gotten worse. . . . Because appeals to you in the past have failed to produce satisfactory change, we have finally lost patience.

We are now sending copies of this letter of complaint, as well as a copy of the previous futile letter, to Mr. Chandler and Mr. Golden at the Columbia University Housing Office in hopes that they, in their official capacities, will be able to take whatever action is required to clean up this long-standing filthy, hazardous condition which you have permitted to develop.

This letter was signed by five tenants and the building superintendent; copies were sent to John Chandler, Columbia's area manager; to Ronald Golden, then director of the Columbia Housing Office; and to the New York City Fire Department, the Department of Health, and the Department of Pest and Rodent Control.

On March 24, Evelyn wrote to her neighbors, "You are quite right, of course, in assuming that three months should be enough" time to clean up; unfortunately, she said, she had only evenings and weekends to work at it. She mentioned that in the course of "disposal and rearrangement" she had discovered a paycheck of four years before, a twenty-dollar bill, and a silver-and-turquoise bracelet, and asked for another month's time to finish the job. One month later, on April 24, she wrote to say she was "not ready for inspection by my standards," and asked her neighbors to be patient rather than renew their complaints.

BUREAU OF FIRE INVESTIGATION
F.D.N.Y.

4th Alarm #1406
Location: 547 Riverside Drive Borough: Man.
Date: 3/2/83 Day: Wed. Time: 10:48
Weather: Windy—W to E

Examination and investigation disclosed that the fire originated on the 6th Floor, in Apt. 6C, in the area of bedrooms No. 1 and No. 2 and extended throughout the entire apartment and up into the cockloft; further extended via cockloft and pipe voids in walls down to Apt. 6D, throughout the entire apt.; further extended down to Apt. 5D, Bedroom No. 1 in NE corner of Apt.; further extending downward via void in front wall of building (west wall) to Apt. 4C (living room) further downward to Apt. 3C (living room) and was there confined and extinguished.

NOTE: Roof of building collapsed into Apts. 6C and 6D. Apt. 6C had extremely heavy fire load throughout apt. (Apt. had cartons of books throughout.)

Signed: Supervising Fire Marshal

According to the *New York Times,* twenty-two firemen out of the 120 responding to the four-alarm blaze were injured, and most of them were treated at St. Luke's–Roosevelt Medical Center nearby. One fireman quoted in the *New York Post* said, "It was like a flamethrower. The flames came right at you." Also from the *Post,* on March 3, 1983: "The fire began at 10:50 A.M. in a sixth-floor apartment that was strewn with debris and garbage, officials said. 'It was piled six feet high,' said Battalion Chief George Bauer. 'You name it and it was in the apartment—milk boxes, newspapers, a collection of automobile jacks. You could name almost anything and they've got it up there.' "

4 Out in the Cold

On the morning of March 2, 1983, our family was scattered, and only our niece Gwen, a college student, remained in the apartment. I had taken a temporary teaching job at the University of Iowa, in Iowa City, for two semesters; our older daughter, Rachel, was away at college; and our younger, Miranda, was staying with friends till I returned in May. Harry had left the apartment the night before and flown out to Iowa City to spend the remaining two months. In the morning our phone began to ring. Half a dozen friends and neighbors could describe the flames vividly, but no one could tell us if Gwen, who slept soundly and late, had gotten out in time. We called Tom Kelly, who was somehow answering his phone in the basement. He promised to look for Gwen and to call back as soon as he had located her, but in the confusion it was two hours until we learned she was safe. Harry flew back to New York that afternoon to be with Gwen and Miranda and to have a look at our apartment.

Meanwhile, in the late afternoon the tenants were allowed inside to survey the damage and retrieve things. The hall windows had been punched out, and a crew of workmen was beginning to board them up with plywood. The hall floors were black and wet and strewn with dirt, debris, and household possessions. The walls were scarred black with smoke, and everywhere was the rancid odor of smoke and damp. Rebecca Rikleen remembers "a tremendous feeling of humidity and ominousness." And as people went into their separate apartments, it became very quiet.

The fire, which according to the fire marshal's report began in 6C, had spread over into 6D and down, damaging most severely the top two floors of the north side—the C and D apartments. Apartment 6C was destroyed, and 6D, the Silversteins' apartment, had disappeared—ragged brick walls stood against the sky. Parts of the floor and ceiling of 6D had collapsed into 5D below, which belonged to Brandon Maggart, who was away in Hollywood, working on a TV situation comedy series. The Maggarts' apartment was wet, black, and strewn with timber and debris.

Earlier in the day, the Greek contractor whose men had been working in 547 had stopped by to see Diana Angel at her daughter Adrienne's apartment in the next building, and told her, "Mrs. Angel, there's been some damage in your apartment." "Some damage!" she said when she entered. The tub and the toilet were ripped out. The furniture was chopped up. The drawers had been opened and messed. Fabrics stored in a trunk were ruined. Sterling silverware was missing. All her correspondence with Lyndon Johnson was destroyed, as well as family mementos and photographs of her third husband in his splendid Greek naval commander's uniform. Jewelry was missing: earrings, a gold chain, a watch. Also gone were a jade necklace and a string of pearls given to her by her other daughter, Connie.

In the north-wing apartments just below the worst devastation, the tenants found most of their possessions wet and ruined. Furniture was destroyed; pianos were filled with water; the contents of closets were dumped on the floor and wrecked. Most people had no insurance.

As they entered their second-floor apartment on the north side of the building, Joan and Christian Regelin found the back bedrooms not badly damaged. "But as we walked to the front we could hear it raining. The bedroom ceiling—that was our front room, facing the park—had come down and the bed was sopping wet. Water was pouring through the beams. The firemen had put plastic over certain things, over the piano. When I walked into the living room I just stood there for several minutes, not knowing what to take out first. I was totally dazed. Vaguely I thought, Well, the damage is bad, but the piano's intact. I grabbed the kids' violins. The music—that's what I thought of. Christian went around and picked up some things for the children and me. He asked me, 'Where's the jewelry?' These were some family heirlooms my mother-in-law gave me, that we kept in a top drawer in a bedroom dresser and in a cabinet. They were gone."

Across the hall on the south side, only the top floor—6A and 6B—suffered smoke and water damage. For almost two decades, Nena O'Neill had lived in 6B, where she had raised two sons and, together with her husband, written several books. After George, a professor of anthropology at City College, died in 1980, Nena had stayed on alone, going through their papers and trying to work on her own, but she found the memories and the grief too oppressive. So several months before the fire, in an attempt to try writing in a different environment, she had rented a small place downtown to use as an office and begun moving some of her papers there.

"I rushed in after the firemen and found that my door was broken down completely," she recalls. "The first shock—I suppose it's like a burglary or any other total devastation. Broken plaster falling from big holes in the ceiling, debris, water, all in a scramble, everything thrown all over. It looked ransacked. My precious archaeological pieces smashed. My slides—some were strewn all over the floor. I thought, Oh, my God, all those memories of my life, photos of the kids, all charred and ruined. My bed was totally soaked, from the firemen rushing about with hoses. The books were charred, the rugs covered with gobs of wet plaster and dirt. In the study it was utter mayhem—files all over the floor, dirt from the plants. The feeling of violation, the disbelief that anything can so disorder your possessions . . ."

Most of those living on the south wing—the A and B apartments—were more fortunate. Mrs. Lurier's first-floor apartment was intact, as were Inge Irving's (4A) and Rebecca Rikleen's (3A); the parrot and cats Chris had worried about were safe too. "It seemed incredible," Rebecca says. "I had already made peace with the idea of having lost everything, then I went in and it was all there. I had mixed feelings. It was amazing and wonderful that we had all this, but I was guilty too: It seemed unfair that we were spared and other people suffered so much. It *was* unfair. And we couldn't divide it up.

"In a few of the other apartments, like the Maggarts', it was black like after a war, after a bombing, and freezing cold. The amazement of it drew us back to look. What had been homes was just rubble. All the care and loving and warmth was gone. It was a sodden mess."

While a fire truck remained to spray water on the building all night, the tenants arranged for places to sleep. Diana Angel stayed next door with Adrienne; Inge and Victor Irving stayed with Inge's daughter Debby and Debby's roommate, next door to the north, in 548. Rebecca, her thirteen-year-old son Ethan, Chris, Daniel, the two children, the parrot, and the cats slept on the floor of The Red Balloon, Rebecca's day care center, one block north. Joan and Christian Regelin and their three children stayed with Joan's aunt and uncle in Westchester.

The Department of Buildings placed a vacate order on the north wing of 547 the day of the fire; the tenants from the south wing whose apartments were undamaged could not occupy their homes either, since John Chandler, the manager of Columbia University properties in the area, had called various crews of workmen to board up the windows, to stand guard at the entrance, to disconnect the gas and electricity, and to put chains and locks on all the corridor doors leading to the apartments. The following day, March 3, the eight tenants affiliated with Columbia—teachers, graduate students, and their families—were helped to find new and nearby apartments by the university, which owns and manages about 4,800 apartments in Morningside Heights.

Immediately after Harry went to the building on the morning of March 3, he called the Columbia Housing Office. "I asked what they were going to do about it. A woman said, 'If you need any help why don't you call us?' Well, I was calling, so I asked again about their plans. I said, Isn't anyone going to come over to talk with us about where to get apartments, as they were doing for their affiliated tenants? Chandler was there, but he had no answers; the fire insurance people were there with Columbia officials, but no one was saying a word to the tenants about what was happening. They weren't planning to meet with us at all, as far as I could discern, and people were milling around in a state of shock, with no place to live. And it was common knowledge that they're the third-largest landlord in the city, after the city itself and the Catholic Church; also that with their thousands of apartments there are usually a good many vacancies at any one time. Well, finally the woman said someone would be there later that day. I got the feeling that if I hadn't called nothing would have happened.

"I figured we needed help. I spoke to a few people—Inge, Joan. We made a list." Harry then called the offices of State Assemblyman Ed Sullivan, State Senator Franz Leichter, City Councilman

Fred Samuel, City Council President Carol Bellamy, Senators Patrick Moynihan and Alfonse D'Amato, Congressman Ted Weiss, and Borough President Andrew Stein.

"I said we wanted to make sure we got some accommodations, the same as the affiliates, and that the building was rebuilt. I emphasized the shock of it, the fact that it was winter and the building was closed and we needed help. We wanted to be sure everyone had a place to stay that night. They were all very concerned and willing to help. Leichter's office said someone would come to the meeting that afternoon. Ed Ortiz from Weiss's office came to a couple of meetings. Earl Brown from Stein's office came several times too. And they all said they'd write letters."

Columbia sent Larry Dais, director of community affairs, to meet with the tenants of 547 Riverside Drive on March 3 in Inge Irving's apartment, 4A, which was undamaged. "When we sat there," Inge says, "it was like nothing had happened in the rest of the building." Dais brought along Joe Kern of New York City's Department of Relocation; three of the eight Columbia-affiliated tenants came as well. (The affiliates helped their former neighbors during the first two weeks in March. "We didn't see any more of them after that," Harry says.)

The tenants' perceptions of this first representative of the university are curiously diverse: unctuous and condescending, courteous and considerate, hostile and defensive. There was uniformity, however, in their interpretation of the message Dais brought about plans for the building. "They were not answering any questions," Harry remembers. "They said if it gets rebuilt we'll go back, but they wouldn't say if it would be rebuilt or when we would know, only that their engineers would look at it. They wanted to turn us over to the city, which offers welfare hotels, and then the possibility of getting into public housing."

Mr. Kern of the Department of Relocation suggested accommodations at the Martinique Hotel on West Thirty-second Street, a shoddy refuge for the homeless and transient, which Inge Irving immediately called an insult. As it happened, her indignation was irrelevant, since she and the other tenants from the relatively undamaged south wing were ineligible for city aid: their side of the building was not under any Buildings Department vacate order.

Nevertheless, the tenants, at least those from the south wing, were slightly encouraged by that first meeting, and hoped that after some cleaning up and checking of the utilities, they might be back in their homes. They also hoped that meanwhile they might be housed in university-owned apartments along with their Columbia-affiliated neighbors.

Before the next meeting with Columbia, and all meetings thereafter, the tenants would get together on their own to make sure everyone had a place to stay and to go over individual problems. "Among all of us," Harry says, "was a mood of shock and disbelief, a feeling of, We're going to get through this, we're going to cooperate and help each other."

The hopes raised on March 3 were stifled on March 4 at a second meeting with Columbia representatives held in Inge's apartment, and attended also by State Assemblyman Ed Sullivan, who has a long history of advocating tenants' rights on Morningside Heights. Sullivan urged that the university not profit by a disaster to help ease its own acute housing shortage. "We want to make sure nobody benefits from the accident lest someone get the wrong impression. . . . We've been through enough problems to know there's a lot of vacant housing."

Similarly, Councilman Fred Samuel wrote on March 4 to Michael Sovern, president of Columbia University, stressing that while the residents of 547 Riverside Drive included both affiliated and nonaffiliated tenants, Columbia should "adopt a policy which will demonstrate an equal commitment to *all* of the families who have been victimized by this tragic fire, and . . . provide temporary shelter and other appropriate relief to all of the tenants." Samuel added that he expected the university to rehabilitate the apartments for the affected residents as quickly as possible.

But the university's position, as stated by Larry Dais and quoted three days later in a front-page article in the *Columbia Daily Spectator,* was: "There is responsibility on the University's part to provide emergency relief for students, faculty and staff, but there is no policy to say we should" for non-affiliates. On the subject of vacant apartments, Dais responded that real estate was not his area, but promised that a representative from the Housing Office would meet with the tenants soon.

That representative was Daniel Rosenblatt, Housing Office director, who appeared at a third meeting, on March 7—not in Inge's apartment but in the lobby of 530 Riverside Drive, next door: Columbia announced that 547 was too dangerous, and refused to send its officials there. Rosenblatt, whose area was housing, said he could not answer questions about the future of the building and about temporary housing because he was "not a policymaker." When a tenant reported that Gregory Fusco, vice-president for government relations and community affairs, had said on the phone that morning that the university had decided against offering temporary quarters, Rosenblatt replied, "Yes, that's true." Later he added, "I hope you didn't think I was trying to deceive you." Fusco's position was also quoted in the *Spectator,* which covered the aftermath of the fire with keen attention: "In a housing stock of 4200 units on Morningside Heights, I'm sure there are spaces available. The question is do we change policy."

On its editorial page, the *Spectator,* which is written and edited by students, commented on the policy of refusing to rent apartments to citizens not affiliated with the university, even in an emergency situation:

> Is this a policy Columbia can live with?
>
> No.
>
> The University is not just a landlord. It is a nonprofit educational institution dedicated to humanistic ideas higher than "survival of the fittest." College students should not spend their first two years of their education learning about the humanities and our contemporary civilization so we can say, "life's rough." . . . The . . . non-affiliated people living in 13 of the 21 apartments are as much a part of the community as the students, faculty and staff. Some of them have been living there for more than 20 years. . . . If Columbia does not guarantee housing for the people in those units . . . it would be using the fire to smoke out non-affiliates from its housing. And to what end? A less diverse community, further deteriorated relations with the community—and the suffering of those families unaffiliated with the University.

"After that third time, they wouldn't meet with us," Harry says. "I called Dais, but he wouldn't answer any questions of substance for about two and a half or three weeks. Stonewalling, it's called, as in Watergate."

Selma Silverstein hadn't been eager to go to Florida, nor had she wanted to leave the cat she was so attached to. But since she had a professional conference to attend there, and Jerry had close family and friends he wanted very much to see, they decided to go. Selma calls it an ill-fated trip. "The weather was cold, we got the flu, it was terrible all the way down the line. Then towards the end it finally got sunny, and we thought we'd wind up in a blaze of glory. Ha! The day of the fire, Wednesday—it was uncanny—I was in bed with a fever, reading *Dingley Falls,* a novel by a friend of ours, Michael Malone, and I happened to be reading the chapter where a character's house burns down. And

I was feeling gloomy about the cat, missing her. I thought of the title of a play, *P.S., Your Cat Is Dead.* When we got to my uncle's house the next day there was a message waiting."

Jerry phoned Inge's apartment, where it happened that the tenants were gathered to discuss the fire. Inge told him how one of the tenants had refused to leave the building until she found their cat, but finally was forced to. "Everything is gone," Inge said. Selma asked, "What about my father's paintings? What about our papers?" "Nothing."

"We couldn't comprehend what 'nothing' meant, when Inge said 'nothing.' We thought in terms of damage. We thought we would find things there."

Inge invited Selma and Jerry to join her and Victor in her daughter Debby's apartment next door, where Yvonne Uehling and her dog were also staying. (Debby moved out to stay with a friend for the time being.) When the Silversteins got off the plane in New York the following day, they found Victor Irving waiting. "He carried our bags. He was sweet and generous and always looking for ways to help. We had no clothes left, only the summer clothes we had taken to Florida, and it was winter in New York. Before she left, Debby had told Inge to show me her closet full of clothes and said, 'Selma can have anything she wants.' Beverly Gros, a neighbor from 548 whom we barely knew, sent us food and clothes. Everyone was bringing food."

On the evening of March 4, Jerry and Selma went to the building, carrying flashlights, with Inge, Debby, and Victor. They had to ask permission of the guard, who unchained the door of the building but warned them not to go past the kitchen of 6D—it was unsafe. "When we got to the sixth-floor landing and saw the cold, blackened hole that was our apartment, we felt such an overwhelming sense of loss and shock. It must be the way people feel after a bombing or an earthquake. I had this immediate sense of what had been where—total recall. I could visualize the whole place and every object had a meaning. Especially my father's paintings. My father was an embroidery machine operator, but after he got cancer and couldn't work anymore, he painted. The loss of the paintings was like losing my father all over again, losing all the things he had made and touched."

The following day, in the hall of 530 Riverside Drive, Jerry met Daniel Rosenblatt and James Kyrimes of the Columbia Housing Office, and Larry Dais. He said to them, "I can't believe that Columbia University is not going to recognize the humanity of the situation. You're the third-largest landlord in the city. You've got to have apartments available for people like us who are thrown into this emergency situation." They answered that all the apartments they had were being repaired. "I couldn't believe people could be so callous to other people's sufferings," Jerry says. "I even called to try to establish affiliation rights through my connection with Teachers College. After all, I had taught there for many years. But they were not very encouraging: the rules and regulations regarding affiliation are very strict. I was rebuffed at every turn."

The fire caught Jerry at a difficult time. He had retired from his job at WNYE, the Board of Education TV station, in 1982 and was about to leave his part-time job teaching speech and broadcasting at Columbia University's Teachers College, in order to return to acting. He had been studying at the Herbert Berghof studio in New York and starting to look for work. In the fire, the résumé he had just prepared was destroyed, along with his photographs. "I was already having roller-coaster emotions at the change—acting is a rejecting profession—and then the fire struck and my life was turned upside down. It seemed everything was ending—my work, my teaching, and now my home."

On March 5, Jerry and Selma called their son Kenny in San

Francisco. They hadn't wanted to trouble Kenny, since he was starting a new job, but when he heard the news he insisted on coming. "This was my home," he said. He, too, would stay in Debby Irving's apartment. And then they bought shovels and a digging fork and began digging to see what they could salvage.

The fire had gone from 6C up to the roof, which collapsed into Jerry's and Selma's apartment, causing parts of their ceiling to collapse into Buddy Maggart's apartment below. In the heat, tar from the roof had melted, becoming flaming pitch, which seared the apartment so intensely that brass and copper objects melted. Then the tar hardened to a black asphalt over the floor, covering everything in the apartment. It was this hardened asphalt that the Silversteins dug through. With no roof, they were exposed to cold and rainy March weather.

Kenny dug systematically from one end of the apartment to the other for four days, and discovered a strongbox that held tax records, checkbooks, and insurance policies. For two days, Selma remembers, "we looked for the brass candlestick my grandmother brought with her from Russia when she came with nine children. The most treasured things she brought were the candlestick, a brass spoon, and a wooden thing she used to pull her washing out of the river. Years ago I found a candlestick exactly like it in an antique shop, with the same Russian letters, and I used them as a pair. Eventually Kenny uncovered this store-bought one, but I like to think it's the one my grandmother carried from Russia in her hand, although I know it's not."

In a smashed china closet they found a pair of porcelain demitasse cups intact. "Firemen do that," Jerry says, "smash everything up to make sure there are no lurking flames or smoke. But imagine those cups surviving! The most delicate little things, a birthday gift. I lost a German sword I got in the war and kept near my bed. I went down to the Maggarts' apartment to see if it might have fallen through the floor. It hadn't, but down there on the walls I saw all the many notes and Valentines from Brandon's children over the years. I wondered whether I ought to save them, then decided I'd better leave them for Brandon to go through himself when he got back from Los Angeles. Later on, a salvage crew sent by the fire department found an empty turtle shell, but they found no trace of the turtles or of their tank. Selma had kept those turtles alive for fifteen years. She had studied all about what to feed them—I never heard of anyone's turtles lasting that long.

"During all this digging I was constantly worried about where we would stay, what we would do in the future, while Selma was more upset over the losses. At any rate, we stayed at Debby's for a week, with Inge in the next room, Debby's roommate in and out, and Kenny there for a while. Victor moved across town to stay with a friend. Then Jonathan Irving, around the corner on Claremont, was going away for three weeks, and so we stayed there. That was not a Columbia building."

The other tenants, too, managed in ad hoc quarters, returning to the building daily to pack up their things and move them out, although with no lights, boarded-up windows, and no elevator, this task was impossible for some. Coula Lurier went to stay with her son Norman in Buffalo, while her son Harold took charge of clearing out her things, as well as his aunt's.

"Our assumption," Harold remembers, "was that we'd be back in soon. And that assumption was kept alive in the first meetings with Dais and Kyrimes. They said, It'll be a few more days. Those next few days we dug, dug, dug. Friends came to dig along with me. In my mother's apartment nothing was destroyed; it was intact. But in my aunt's, on the fifth floor, we dug through debris to get under the rug because she said she had money there. It took a whole day and then there was nothing there. For three days I ran up and down the steps between the two apartments, trying to clear them out and collect the valuables. We packed my aunt's stuff in plastic bags and left them in the lobby, as Columbia said to do, but when she unpacked, lots of things were missing. I'd put stuff outside the door and the next thing I knew it was gone. There were a lot of students running up and down, helping. By the end I was covered with black, my clothes, everything. My cousin Adrienne was prostrate with exhaustion."

While Diana Angel was next door with Adrienne, the university's Office of Investments, run by computer, sent her a rent bill as usual, which she found infuriating, especially after what she regarded as Columbia's negligence in allowing apartment 6C to remain in so cluttered a state. On the other hand, she was touched when two women, aged eighty-two and eighty-four, from her service organization, the Order of the Eastern Star, came to her with money and offers of help, saying that after all the help she had given others, now it was her turn to receive. "They did it that way, with women of my age, so as not to embarrass me as much as I would have been with younger women."

The Red Balloon served as home for Rebecca Rikleen, its director, and her family. "Ethan and I slept on couches. Daniel and Chris and the children slept on gym mats. They all had to be up and out by eight o'clock, which was when the teachers arrived for the day, and their things had to be out of sight till six o'clock. That was very difficult. Daniel, who had just finished medical school, was working in a hospital in New Jersey, so he could go there every day, and the children went to school, but Chris, also a doctor, was waiting for a job to come through, and didn't know where to hang out. She looked at ads for apartments, but they couldn't manage it. Before the fire Ethan often used to come by after school. But this was very different. With the staff around till six, he felt like a guest. We got so used up in our tolerance. He lost his teddy bear there, which was precious to him, and a number of other things. It was hard to keep track of things with all the children around. We had a stove there, we could do minor cooking, but we ate an awful lot of Chinese food during those weeks.

"After a few days Chris and Daniel told Columbia they had nowhere to stay and Columbia put them in the Empire Hotel [on West Sixty-third Street] for one weekend. Then they got city placement in a hotel on Forty-third Street. Then they sublet a place in Washington Heights. They kept moving around.

"You get so unhinged you don't think logically. I kept thinking it would be a month till we were back home. It seemed as if the building was sturdy, and they were not keeping us out, as far as going in to get things and clean up. So I was really hurt that Chris and Daniel left. At the time it seemed we were all in a lifeboat and they had left us there in the lifeboat and gone in another direction. I felt strongly about sticking together in adversity. But as Chris later told me, they didn't feel comfortable there. There was just no place for them.

"We spent days going over to the building to gawk. We would go up and walk through the Silversteins' apartment. The idea that the blackness underfoot was their life's belongings, the idea of being outdoors under the bleak sky and walking over their life's belongings, was so peculiar that I did it a number of times. I gawked at Evelyn Owens' things; there were mounds and shelves full of stuff that was not destroyed, where only the surface had burned off. Evelyn spent time going through burnt crust to get to things—her hands and arms were black like a coal miner's."

Nena O'Neill was now staying in her new office, but went back to the apartment for what she called a "rescue operation." "You react as though you're on emergency call. Like a surge of adrenaline. My only thought was, What do I want to save first?—as if the building were about to fall down. How can I get my books out? Where do I take everything? And the tapes and photos. George was an inveterate photographer—every trip we took. Twenty years of shots from the apartment. Out the window in the snow, the fall, the sunsets. Every event of our lives—birthdays, celebrations, weddings, archaeological trips.

"I hired a group of neighborhood kids to help me. Some of them wiped the shreds of carbon off the photos, others worked on the books. I called the Columbia library to ask how to salvage the books—I remember sitting there on the floor of the burnt apartment, talking about it on the telephone. They said there were special sponges chemically treated to neutralize the acid, but it had to be done soon after the fire. Who had the time to go and buy them? Then I had to find cartons just the right size for the books, not too big, so I could carry them out. Thank God I found commercial storage space. I could never have fit it all in my office. I gave a lot of stuff to the kids helping me, things like a coffeepot, charred but usable, only I didn't have the heart to clean them. It's amazing what fire jumps over; it's so capricious, the nature of flames. Some things it leaves untouched, and yet it manages to besmirch what you really like.

"I would go there wearing old clothes I didn't care about. There was no water. We didn't even know where to pee; finally we peed in the toilets, black as they were. We worked six to eight hours a day. Right after the fire the carbon fragments in the air were at their height. I got sick after about four days. The doctor told me to get a mask. Except for the few days I was sick, I was there every day for about three weeks, lugging, packing, throwing things out. At night I'd strip off all the contaminated clothes and roll them up in a plastic bag. I was so saturated with smoke, I couldn't stand the smell anymore. And as my body got more saturated, so did my emotions. The enormity of what I was doing only hit me each night after the day's work. I'd just break down and cry and say, That's all I needed now, after everything else. I lost my husband, I broke my hip, I got mugged, my car was broken into, and now losing all my possessions, every memory of the past. There were times when I wondered if I'd be able to deal with it; these were times I wished it had been total destruction. Some friends told me to walk out, just leave it all, but I couldn't do that. Even so, I knew I was in an enviable position. I had no insurance, but I had some important files, my typewriter, and most of my writing in the new office. I had a place to go."

A few days after the fire, Nena called the office of Columbia's managing agent for the building, Ronald Golden, and spoke to a woman there who said, "Mrs. O'Neill, who are you? We don't have you listed as a tenant. We only have George O'Neill listed." Nena replied that for twenty years she had been paying the rent with her own checks.

Joan and Christian Regelin and their children spent the first few days after the fire crowded into Joan's aunt's and uncle's house in Westchester, hoping that the building would be promptly repaired. Joan was in the midst of performing several concerts that week, one a memorial for a friend who had died of cancer. "I desperately wanted to do them. Somehow I was able to sing, I don't remember how." And then some close friends who had just moved into a large old farmhouse in New Jersey invited the Regelins to stay with them. Joan considers that these friends "saved our lives as a family." The woman of the family especially, who was a singer at the Metropolitan Opera, gave Joan "another focus," a change of subject from the burned building, the tenant meetings, and the uncertainty about the future.

Still, the arrangement had its problems for a city family of five. "I was spending five hours a day behind the wheel of a car. I would bring Christian in to work and the kids to school in the city at eight o'clock. If I had rehearsals I would stay, if not I would come back. Later in the day I would bring the kids back to New Jersey, and then go back in the evening to perform or attend tenant meetings. They took up such an immense amount of time, and in retrospect I don't know if they were worth a damn. I was literally commuting two or three times a day. It was a wild time. Somehow the kids were able to stay in school, which is incredible when I think of it. I was in the depths of depression."

On March 7, the Monday after the fire, Joan and Christian went to get some things out of the building. "It was then that we found the damage was only beginning. And after that, every time we went back it was worse and worse. It rained into the building for the next three months."

The six-week period from March 1 to April 10, 1983, was a period of record rainfall in New York City: 10.54 inches in March alone, surpassing two previous records set in 1979 and 1869. Rain fell for almost half of the days in that period. On Sunday, April 10, it fell heavily enough to render the *New York Times* poetic, as it likened subway stations to dripping caves. The rain fell through the damaged ceilings of the north wing, from floor down to floor. The eight north-wing apartments on the first to fourth floors suffered their most severe damage not from fire but from water.

The tenants wondered why Columbia did not promptly put a temporary roof on the north wing, but the university said that since parts of the north wing parapet were "in imminent danger of collapse," preparatory work such as removal of debris, construction of scaffolding, and shoring up the shaky parapet had to be done first. Moreover, it was waiting for the advice of its engineers before undertaking any repairs. Despite the "imminent danger of collapse," tenants saw the Columbia engineers almost immediately installed in a makeshift office in a north-wing apartment equipped with water and electricity, not available anywhere else in the building. They feared that the blueprints in evidence were designed to break up the apartments into dormitory rooms for students, given Columbia's housing shortage and its well-known policy of "clearing out" tenants not affiliated with the university. The unanimous instinct was that the landlord was dragging its feet on constructing a new roof in the hopes that with the aid of time and nature, the building might drift past the point of repair.

Throughout March there was a good deal of traffic in the building: not only the university's engineers, workmen, officials, and lawyers, but tenants, their families and helpers, moving men making estimates, insurance agents, and so on. It was a surprise, then, when in the middle of the month there appeared a small document prepared by the university's Office of Real Estate Management, to be signed by all tenants entering the building:

> Columbia University has advised me that by reason of the fire, 547 Riverside Drive is unsafe to enter. I am aware of the great risk to me if I enter the building. Notwithstanding such warning, I desire to enter the building to remove my personal property. I hereby release Columbia University, its agents, servants, and employees and agree to indemnify it from and against any claim, damage, or expense by reason of my entering the building, and/or removing of my property.

The document was administered by a uniformed guard who sat reading a newspaper at a desk set up in the lobby, and occasionally by Anna Flanagan, the superintendent, who also sat in the lobby for eight hours a day, frequently with her youngest grandson keeping her company.

A number of tenants refused to sign. Joan described her resulting experience in an article written for the March 22 *Spectator:*

> I refused to sign and I went to my apartment anyway. Columbia called the cops. And we, assured that Columbia had no right to keep

> us out at their discretion, also called the cops. There was a gathering of police that suggested some kind of felony occurring. Yet all that was happening was that I tried to return to my home. The police let me stay.
>
> The next day the statements were back, only this time around they would not unchain the locks which seal off both sides—damaged and undamaged—of the building. Without a court order, they are locking us out until we absolve them of all liability.

After the attempt to administer the document failed because of the tenants' resistance, Columbia instituted a new ruling, that tenants and their helpers must wear hard hats while in the building. With the array of bright colors available, the hats offered some moments of levity, a masquerade-ball touch in a grim situation. The uniformed guard, Mrs. Flanagan, and her visiting grandchildren were apparently not required to wear them. After a few weeks—perhaps the north-wing parapet was sufficiently stabilized—the hats disappeared from the lobby.

All during the month of March, Harry kept writing notes to Larry Dais asking whether the university would relax its policy and allow unaffiliated tenants to use vacant apartments temporarily; when the engineers' reports would be completed; and what plans existed for the restoration and reoccupancy of the building. Legally, Columbia was not bound to provide temporary housing for its burned-out tenants. However, if the university rebuilt 547, it would be required by law to allow the tenants to return to their rent-controlled apartments and to remain for as long as they wished. Those apartments, though hardly luxurious, were old-fashioned six- and seven-room units with high ceilings, two bathrooms, a river view, and moderate rents; no sane New Yorker would give them up or, it seemed to the tenants, watch them vanish without a struggle. The notes also suggested forming a group of university officials, tenants, and elected representatives to review progress and disseminate accurate information, to counter rumors about plans for the site. For example, when I called the Housing Office on March 17 to ask about protecting belongings still in our apartment, James Kyrimes refused to speak with me, but a woman there said that as far as she knew, the building was going to be demolished. The response to the notes was, "I'll let you know."

5 Company Town

Over the past ten years, Columbia University has been beset by more urgent demands for housing than ever before from faculty, students, and staff. In the past, Columbia people might choose to live anywhere in upper Manhattan, within easy reach of the university, or even raise their families in Westchester, Rockland, or Long Island suburbs. But those outlying communities now seem less desirable than they did a few decades ago, and the costs of their housing have become exorbitant. Rents for Manhattan apartments are at absurdly inflated levels too, while the ubiquitous and rapid metamorphosis of rental buildings into cooperatives excludes people without substantial cash to invest. Increasingly, students and employees alike look to the university to provide not only education, jobs, and tenure, but reasonably priced housing as well.

The academic world, no less than the corporate, competes strenuously for talent and brains. If Columbia is to maintain its academic stature, it needs to supply adequate housing. Happily or not, the university, like many other nonprofit institutions, finds itself a large-scale landlord, with more than the usual attendant headaches. A huge staff is needed to run the business, from financial experts brooding over the rate of return on real-estate investments, to building managers responsible for leaky faucets. The professional outlooks of the real-estate people have little in common with those of the faculty and students over whose personal lives they exert so much control. The aims of the institution itself are sadly divided—like guns and butter, profits and intellectual achievement are hard to attain simultaneously—so that within the university the results are mounting frustration and conflict. And in the surrounding neighborhood, Columbia has come to be perceived less as a shining centerpiece enhancing community life than as a threatening and rapacious landlord. Long-term local residents and former Columbia affiliates, equally hard pressed, hang on to their university-owned apartments with extraordinary tenacity, and occasional deviousness.

According to city records available in July 1983, Columbia owned 148, or 49 percent, of the 305 residential buildings in Morningside Heights, the roughly half-square-mile area around the university, bounded by West 110th Street, Riverside Drive, West 125th Street, and Morningside Drive. This means 4,800, or almost 40 percent, of the apartments in the neighborhood. In a University Senate report, these residential holdings are divided by desirability into three categories: the "Gold Coast," which is Riverside Drive and Claremont Avenue; 560 Riverside Drive, a new high-rise building; and Morningside Drive and "other." A little more than a third of the apartments were rented to students, about a quarter to faculty and staff, and slightly less than a third to non-affiliates, that is, local people unconnected with the university, who were living in the buildings when Columbia bought them, and whose continued tenancy is protected by New York State rent regulations. Over 200, or roughly 4 percent, of the university-owned apartments were vacant, which seems a puzzlingly large number in light of the near-desperate situation the university claims to exist; according to Columbia's Office of Real

Estate Management, a number of these are being renovated, and presumably some are being held for faculty and students soon to arrive. In addition to apartments, the university owns or controls 2,160, or 60 percent, of the single-room-occupancy (SRO) units in the community, which it rents mostly to students.

This great quantity of "housing stock" is a fairly recent development. In February 1977, Columbia owned about 3,000 apartments; over six years it increased its holdings by almost two-thirds. The university's most common practice is to purchase occupied buildings and gain space either through legal maneuvers (eviction of part-time faculty or of those no longer affiliated) or attrition (as non-affiliates die or move out, renting only to affiliated tenants).*

A turning point for Morningside Heights was the 1974 *Sperling* court decision resulting from a landlord-tenant dispute and seen as a misfortune or a liberation, depending on one's side of the fence. *Sperling* has since been read as exempting Columbia from rent-control and rent-stabilization guidelines in cases of apartments rented to affiliates, that is, as allowing Columbia to treat its residential buildings as dormitories. (Both rent control and rent stabilization place limits on permitted rates of rent increases, with the former originally more stringent—the difference has been narrowing lately, however. Rent control applies to tenants who have been in residence since before June 30, 1971; it further ensures that they cannot be evicted. The burned-out tenants in 547 Riverside Drive were living under rent control. In today's urban market, tenants under either type of regulation are decidedly fortunate.)

Not surprisingly, Columbia began raising the rents of affiliated tenants at rates that seemed capricious at best. From 1978 to 1982, Columbia's rent increases for affiliates compounded to 60

*At intervals, the meaning of "affiliated" has been redefined more narrowly, thus excluding tenants who believed their continued occupancy was guaranteed.

percent, compared to 44 percent for ordinary New York City tenants living under rent stabilization. For the decade from 1970 to 1980, census figures show Morningside Heights to have experienced the fastest rate of increase in rents in Manhattan: 250 percent, outstanding even nationwide. The university also began offering its affiliates only one-year leases—which meant rents could be raised annually—rather than the choice of one-, two-, or three-year leases prescribed under rent stabilization. And yet with all that, Columbia's reported return on real-estate investments failed to increase.

The havoc and hardships such measures brought to the lives of graduate students and teachers, particularly junior faculty, are amply documented. A 1982 letter to the provost opens:

> You must be weary of such letters, but I feel compelled to write. I am a second year Assistant Professor. Each month I take home $1,192.00 and each month give back to Columbia over 55% or $660.00 for rent. We have three children, ages six, three and a half, and four months, and my wife earns no income. . . . Sadly, in the one area over which we have no control, we are subject to yearly rental increases which are, given my salary and the number of persons it must support, unreasonable and it seems to me, unjust. . . . It is the single pressure coming from the University and its housing policy which will make our condition desperate.

And from a senior faculty member:

> I recently received notice of an increase in the rent for my apartment . . . of 11 per cent. Almost at the same time I received notice of a cost of living salary increase of 5 per cent. The result of the two notices is that after taxes the salary increase just about covers the rent increase. This leaves me behind in all the other increases in prices that have occurred this year—which amounted to 8.9 per cent in 1981 and has run about 7 per cent for the first half of 1982.
>
> In the 18 years that I have been at Columbia, the rent has gone up 2.6 times. My salary has gone up 2.19 times.

These laments represented the experiences of many faculty members. What made their frustration more galling was the realization that they might have pursued their careers at universities less harrowed by real-estate pressures. A professor with a wife and two young children writes:

> To be honest I must add that the whole housing situation here makes me view Columbia with a very limited time-horizon. Theoretically tenure means I can stay here until retirement, but in practical terms I can stay here until my two children begin to explode out of their tiny bedroom. If I had taken my other tenure offers . . . this would not have been the case.

And from the senior professor quoted above:

> I understood that tenants in New York City had a choice of a three-year lease that would entail an increase of no more than 17 per cent over the three years. . . . But the fact is that tenured faculty who are committed to Columbia end up taking a beating. Tenured faculty are in effect treated worse than ordinary citizens. . . .
>
> Last year I was offered a distinguished professorship with a substantial increase in salary at a sun-belt university where the cost of living would be much less. I turned it down. But having had salary increases of only 5 per cent and rent increases of 11 per cent two years running makes me feel, quite frankly, very insecure. What is tenure worth—and the personal commitment that faculty like me have made to Columbia over these many years—if we are so vulnerable that our position can be totally destroyed by just a very few years of salary increases well below the increase in cost of living and rent increases well in excess of it?

Before World War II, a relatively laissez-faire attitude prevailed in the regulation of housing, which is a form of private property. But in the 1940s the New York State legislature declared a housing emergency, which was reiterated in 1983. Since then the rights normally pertaining to private property have been severely limited in the case of housing: the law recognizes it as a public necessity that cannot be left to individual and arbitrary arrangements. Certain practices remain unregulated, however. Landlords are still permitted to keep apartments empty, as in the case of Columbia's more than two hundred vacancies, even amidst a shortage. Deliberate vacancies are common throughout New York City right now, despite the desperately tight situation, since landlords who anticipate their buildings going co-op wait out the process for more lucrative sales. The right to keep apartments vacant while so many are homeless is, in the view of Kenny Schaeffer, a tenant lawyer on Morningside Heights, an anachronism based on obsolete notions of private property. "An analogy," he says, "would be hoarding water in time of a shortage." He also notes the anomaly of landlords with vacant apartments being permitted to raise the rents on others: "They shouldn't be able to plead that they need more money if they have apartments they could be renting."

In the early 1980s, a number of institutional landlords besides Columbia took advantage of court decisions exempting them from rent stabilization and proceeded to demand very high rents or to evict long-term tenants and use the space for institutional purposes. A fact sheet prepared by the Coalition of Tenants of Non-Profit Institutional Landlords, a group seeking legislative remedies in Albany, cites not only Columbia but the Museum of Modern Art, Syracuse University, Mount Sinai Hospital, and Presbyterian Hospital; tentative moves in the same direction have been made by Jewish Theological Seminary, Gracie Square Hospital, Lenox Hill Hospital, and others. Naturally, when one institution wins a favorable decision in court, the others tend to use it as a license for similar practices. Thus after the Slavin–Syracuse University case of 1982, in which Syracuse won a ruling sympathetic to its real-estate needs, Columbia notified non-affiliated tenants in recently purchased buildings that they were no longer protected by rent stabilization and would thenceforth be offered only one-year leases.

These institutions' mission of serving the public good and their best interests as entrepreneurs are at cross-purposes. In the latter role, their legal position is based on a provision of the 1974 Emergency Tenant Protection Act intended to exempt any property owned by monasteries, universities, hospitals, and the like from rent stabilization. (A 1983 amendment exempted only such property rented to the institutions' affiliates, however, leaving those tenants unprotected.) Yet as its name suggests, the legislation was not originally enacted to oust families or disrupt neighborhoods. At a June 1983 Morningside Heights community meeting, local sentiments were aptly expressed by an SRO tenant involved in a dispute with Columbia: he said that while the university's School of Social Work teaches methods of alleviating social problems, and its Presbyterian Hospital exists to make sick people well, the rental policies of both create social ills and make well people sick.

In the late 1970s, senior professors at Columbia began to feel as pressed as their junior colleagues, what with increases occurring annually, post-*Sperling,* at a rate nearly double that of salaries. Those close to retirement dreaded a drop in income and relentlessly ascending rents. They were also concerned that if things continued in the same way, before long Morningside Heights would no longer be their treasured and affordable academic enclave, where Broadway seems a cross between a highly sophisticated Main Street and a Mediterranean bazaar. Not least among the factors spreading discontent was the way the University Housing Office treated its clientele—with "arbitrariness, favoritism, discourtesy, and inefficiency."

Indignation among faculty ultimately led to the Senate Panel on Housing and Rental Policy, composed of seven professors, one administrator, and two graduate students. This group's Final Report (from which the preceding quotations from faculty members are taken) was made public on March 21, 1983, less than three weeks after fire devastated 547 Riverside Drive. The fire was not mentioned in the Final Report, nor were any of the problems of 1,667 non-affiliated tenants, one-third of the total number of people who call Columbia landlord. This was not an oversight; the panel's specific task was simply "To study the rental properties of the University with respect to the conflict between the University's need to earn a reasonable rate of return on its investments and its need to provide local and affordable housing to faculty, students, and staff."

However, in the context of the well-known frustration over Columbia-owned housing, such a purpose for a panel on housing policies struck local residents as willfully narrow. Nowhere in the Final Report is there any awareness that the university is supported and enlivened by a variegated urban population of thousands who were living on Morningside Heights years before the university went into the real-estate business. On the contrary, the report gives an impression of the Heights as an enclosed campus on which a number of unwelcome aliens are usurping space. In the words of Tom Kappner of the Morningside Tenants Federation, a neighborhood action group which requested to no avail to be represented on the Senate's subcommittee on housing, the report was "formulated in a vacuum." (In a more heated moment, the usually mild-mannered Kappner likened Columbia president Michael Sovern to a "feudal baron.")

The report placed the blame for the university's problems—the shortage of space, high rent increases, and low profits—not on bureaucratic inefficiency or poor financial management, but on the non-affiliated tenants' paying low (rent-controlled or rent-stabilized) rates. It reproached the administration for:

> the failure to eject non-affiliated tenants when the renter and spouse had died or relocated; the same failure in the case of affiliated tenants; and, most important, the retention of apartments by persons whose affiliation with Columbia no longer entitled them to University housing. Several years ago, the Administration organized itself to attack this problem aggressively, but the effort was not sustained. Estimates of the number of "illegal" tenants vary. Some are as high as 1000; the lowest are in the 400 to 500 range. Since the stepped-up effort was launched in 1980 about 100 apartments have been recaptured. Admittedly the process of recapture from initial identification to voluntary release or legal eviction requires diligence and sensitivity, but the record to date speaks more to avoidance, indifference, and lack of energy on the part of the officialdom, with no participation or help of other members of the Columbia family who have knowledge of changes of status implying loss of affiliation.

Because of passages such as this, local response to the Final Report was outrage; the Reverend William Sloane Coffin of The Riverside Church found it "interesting that students and faculty don't realize how arrogant they appear to the outside world."

Columbia responded to the report's rebuke by embarking on another "stepped-up effort"; throughout the remainder of 1983 and in early 1984, many part-time faculty members and former affiliates received letters ordering them to vacate their homes or face eviction within thirty days.

The panel proposed a number of measures that would equalize the rents for affiliates in comparable apartments and not place additional burdens on junior faculty and those near retirement, nor drive away desirable future teachers and students. It also suggested that the Housing Office tell the truth and improve its manners. Of greater pertinence to the community was the counsel of "early and aggressive action to reduce the gross discrepancies that currently exist between the rents of non-affiliated and affiliated tenants . . . perhaps the single most important factor responsible for the relatively low return on the University's housing stock."

And yet these discrepancies are seen by Columbia's critics as a self-imposed paradox. As Assemblyman Ed Sullivan, his aide Kenny Schaeffer, and others have pointed out, non-affiliates pay relatively low rents because they have been living in their apartments for so long. Since Columbia no longer rents on the open market, it cannot enjoy the rent increases new unaffiliated tenants would bring. If the university were to set aside a portion of its holdings for ordinary tenants, conceivably people would move about more often and more readily. With a natural turnover of apartments, rents could be profitably and legally raised at each turnover. And with more income thus generated, the university might not have to charge its own people such painful rates. Moreover, if the university rented apartments in adjacent neighborhoods such as Manhattan Valley or the Upper West Side and sublet them to faculty, the shortage would be further eased. And if the university did not make costly and lengthy renovations each time an apartment was vacated—renovations even the panel suspected are undertaken less out of necessity than to justify high increases—there would not be 238 vacancies while professors and students plead for apartments.

The other panel recommendation that threatened and incensed local people was the "surveillance" urged on all members of the university, to reduce "slippage."

> The University should strengthen its surveillance of the present occupants in its buildings to assure that those who do not meet its criteria for continued occupancy be required to vacate. On the basis of the evidence that we were able to review, stricter surveillance could result in the recapture of several hundred apartments. Considerable slippage appears to occur when faculty and other affiliated tenants shift from full-time to part-time status. Full-time University work should be the

> basic criterion of affiliation. All officials of the University who have knowledge of the changes in the affiliation status of tenants can contribute to the integrity of the system by making such information available to the rental authorities.

Accordingly, the updated *University Housing Policies and Procedures,* published in the spring of 1984, reinforces the notion of surveillance.

> A computer system provides routine verification of the status of tenants through automated links to the University's personnel and student registration information files. Implementation of this updating program can be improved if members of the University community who know of changes in the affiliation status of tenants or of any other violation of a lease continue to notify the Office of Real Estate Management.

What surveillance means in practice is this: Imagine I am a Columbia professor and for ten years have lived cordially next door to a couple, both in their late sixties, who own a stationery store two blocks away and who were living in their apartment before the university purchased the building. Five years ago their widowed daughter and her children moved in with them. The elderly couple die within a year of each other. I am expected to inform the Office of Real Estate Management so that the daughter and her family can be ejected and the apartment "recaptured." Or suppose that I am a young female graduate student and have grown friendly with the woman next door, the thirty-one-year-old wife of an assistant professor whom she helped put through graduate school, and the mother of three children who attend the local kindergarten and nursery school. One day the professor leaves her and moves in with another woman. I am expected to notify the Office of Real Estate Management so that her apartment can be "recaptured" for use by another Columbia affiliate. (Technically, her husband could be expected to inform on her himself.) Upstairs live a couple in their mid-thirties. The husband wants to try, perhaps for a couple of years, teaching one university course rather than three; he hopes to write a book, or to spend more time with his children while his wife goes back to her interrupted career. But a shift from full-time to part-time status could mean that their apartment is ripe for "surveillance" and "recapture," what Tom Kappner calls "policies which are destroying the fabric of community life."

The recent "stepped-up" enforcement of the "affiliation clause" (that paragraph in the lease granting the apartment only for as long as the occupant works at Columbia full-time) is made even more harsh by the laxity of earlier years. For example, a former Columbia librarian who left his university job in 1969 remained in his apartment with his wife and children until 1982, at which time the affiliation clause was invoked and he was asked to move out. The court upheld the university and issued an eviction warrant. Many such cases exist, in which former graduate students or staff keep their apartments for years, raising families and putting down roots in the neighborhood; during all that time they receive and pay Columbia's rent bills, assuming that the affiliation clause is a technicality not to be taken seriously. Then one day, perhaps as part of a "stepped-up effort," the eviction notice arrives; they grasp that what they have come to regard as home, Columbia has lately chosen to regard as a dormitory.

In June of 1983 the Morningside Tenants Federation presented President Sovern with a petition signed by one thousand people, asking Columbia to stop enforcing the affiliation clause against long-standing residents, not only because it disrupts individual lives and families, but because it destabilizes the neighborhood. The response was even greater efforts of surveillance.

The affiliation clause is one instance out of many in which the university and the community take polarized positions in their tug-of-war over some thirty-five square blocks of mostly old and often shabby residential buildings in an animated and well-located part of New York City. In 1980 the Advisory Board on Residential Housing Policies and Management was founded as a forum where the two sides might talk civilly and seek mutually agreeable solutions. Its members are local leaders and Columbia officials who meet in a somber conference room of The Riverside Church to engage in what was originally conceived of as "an ongoing dialogue" and what the chairman, Tom Kappner, now calls a "ritual exchange of positions."

At the Advisory Board meetings, Columbia's response to the suggestions of community members—for example, that the university guarantee the rights of unaffiliated tenants under rent stabilization, or that it allow local representation on the Senate subcommittee for housing policy—has been twofold: either avoidance, with the vague promise to take them under consideration, or anger that tenants pursue litigation downtown or legislative relief upstate. Community leaders counter with a "we are forced to take care of our own" attitude. More and more people bearing the dreaded letters from Columbia's Office of Real Estate Management seek the help of Assemblyman Sullivan's office and of organizations like the Morningside Tenants Federation in fighting for their homes.

Both sides agree that housing problems cannot be viewed in purely economic terms but demand a broader context. For local leaders that means attention to neighborhood roots and history, and to commercial and recreational patterns; it means a respect for the diverse ethnic and social character of the area, with provisions for nurturing that character. For the university, the broad context is its stature as a seat of learning, implying provisions for attracting and keeping the personnel who can maintain that stature. Repeatedly, activists and bureaucrats find each other intransigent and insensitive, and discussions of general policy end with little more than sore feelings all around.

Community response to the Senate Panel's Final Report had no influence on the university's stance. At a January 1984 Advisory Board meeting, Claude Morton, vice-president for real-estate investments, asked how Columbia could be expected to relax its policies when "we cannot provide for our own faculty and students." And in February, Albert Rosenthal, former dean of the Law School and chairman of the Senate subcommittee on housing, was quoted, in a *Spectator* article headed "CU Must Clear Out Non-Affiliates," as saying that "Columbia is not doing enough to evict non-affiliated tenants." Those students who speak out in favor of tenants' interests, Rosenthal said, "indulge in emotional sympathy, which is unnecessary"; he chastised their "misguided" concern for evicted tenants and their support of the notion that Columbia designate a portion of its housing for non-affiliates. "There's a message that isn't getting through to our people: how vital it is to Columbia to acquire all the housing it can."

Assemblyman Sullivan responded in a letter to the *Spectator:*

> What kind of cynical education is this gentleman trying to give the young people of Columbia? The University Housing Office has disrupted the lives of literally hundreds of people who never have had any affiliation with the University. The Housing Office has taken the attitude, "You're in my way—beat it!" The nadir was reached last year when a mentally ill woman and her aged mother were actually put out on a bench on Broadway. If Mr. Rosenthal thinks this is acceptable behavior for Columbia University, it is to their credit that many students don't agree.
>
> The attitude expressed by Mr. Rosenthal does enormous harm to the University. Why, after all, are his law school colleagues entitled to privileged housing at the expense of someone else's eviction? Can't

these learned people find their way to work on the bus or subway like millions of others do in this city every day? If the Columbia Housing Office would develop the ability to find rentals for senior University people in the many fine communities around the city that are within easy commute to Columbia—Chelsea, Greenwich Village, the West Side, Riverdale, Inwood, the East Side, etc., etc.—then we would have two benefits—a University community that is in full touch with the entirety of this bountiful, resourceful city and peace on Morningside Heights.

May I appeal to students to ignore the cynicism of Mr. Rosenthal and allow your human values to express themselves whenever you see little guys being pushed around by big guys. Maybe your pressure will help bring the University to its senses.*

After the fire in 547, the tenants followed news of housing policies in the *Spectator* with vigilance. When Inge Irving read Rosenthal's statements there, she commented, "Is this what they teach in law school, how to screw people? It shows a total disregard for the community. Universities have charters—an obligation to the community is part of the charter. How dare they make these statements to young people?"

She was particularly offended as she recalled her own contributions to the life of the neighborhood. "P.S. 36, the school on Amsterdam Avenue—why, that was dreamed up in my kitchen. Columbia wanted a new school in the district. They wanted it for their faculty's children, an experimental school, really a private

*This letter was not published, but the *Spectator* did print a response from Tom Kappner of the Morningside Tenants Federation, similarly expressing "amazement and dismay" at Rosenthal's remarks. A week later, the letters column carried a reply from a "troubled" Rosenthal, saying that his comments had been misstated in the original article: "Tenants who antedated Columbia's acquisition of an apartment house are . . . legally and ethically entitled to retain their apartments and neither I nor anyone that I know in the University proposes to evict them." He closed the lengthy re-explanation of his views with the point that "the presence of Columbia people" had saved Morningside Heights both from becoming a slum and from becoming gentrified.

school paid for by public funds. We fought this. We got four thousand signatures and went to Albany and got a trade-off. It was built on public land in Morningside Park. Now it's a community school, the first kindergarten-to-third-grade in the borough. Ben worked on this too.

"Our three kids all went to P.S. 125 [the local elementary school] and Debby went to P.S. 43 [the local junior high]. I was active in the Parents Association, and on the local community planning board. During the teachers' strikes in 1968, when Victor was in elementary school, I helped set up an alternative school on 126th Street, across from the police precinct station. In all this I was going to meetings with the heads of Teachers College, of all the institutions. We had to teach morality to people who are the heads of moral institutions. Everything I worked for in this neighborhood is related to integrating the community—I don't mean racially; it's always been very mixed—I mean the university and the residents. What they're doing is the opposite of integrating. A community in order to be healthy has to have everyone. We're steady, not just there for two or three years. The steady part makes it good for everyone. And our particular mix was the best anyone could have—old, young, some on welfare, some who could have lived elsewhere, some professionals, all politically very different, all colors."

The Red Balloon, the cooperative day care center directed since 1972 by Rebecca Rikleen, is one example of the "steady part." It is housed in 560 Riverside Drive, a new high-rise built by the New York State Dormitory Authority for Columbia; despite its ungainly, fortress-like appearance, 560 is a swank building for Morningside Heights, with its accoutrements of doorman, parking garage, security system, picture windows, and comely lobby. Aside from the donation of space, The Red Balloon is not funded by Columbia or any of the other institutions in a prodigiously institutional area (The Riverside Church, Union Theological Seminary, Jewish Theological Seminary, Barnard College, St. Luke's Hospital, Bank Street College of Education, The Manhattan School of Music) but subsists on tuition and serves the children of faculty members along with those of local black, white, Hispanic, and Asian-American families.

Rebecca formerly worked as a public school teacher, as well as a counselor and nurse in summer camps. "The Red Balloon began," she recalls, "when Ethan was small. I was sharing child care with another mother who was a Ph.D. student at Columbia. We would talk about starting a day care center, and soon we started going to planning meetings involving Columbia and Teachers College. Space for a day care center had been built into 560—there were three classrooms—but it was being used as part of the controller's office. There were lots of meetings, but they didn't seem to get anywhere. At some point it appeared to us that if we simply asked for the space and said we'd do the work, we'd get it. And so we did. Five mothers did it collectively; we started with ten children, several from 560 and others from the neighborhood. People donated equipment, built furniture, gave their time. It was a bootstrap operation and grew to forty-five kids with three teachers and three assistant teachers, and a program that goes from eight-thirty to five-thirty. We still run it as a co-op, and the only money we get is a city subsidy for some kids whose parents can't afford to pay."

Columbia's behavior as a landlord in regard to Rebecca illustrates the ironies in its stance towards the community. Although the university provides space for the day care center so useful to its faculty members, it would not tell its director when she might be permitted back in her apartment, which suffered no damage in the March 2 fire. Nor would it offer her—or her fellow tenants—temporary living quarters in 560. Were Rebecca seeking to move to Morningside Heights now, Columbia would not rent to her because she is not technically affiliated with the university. Rather, despite their efforts on behalf of the neighborhood, Rebecca, Inge, and others like them are the sorts of tenants whom the university hopes in time to "clear out."

At a November 1983 meeting of the Advisory Board, Assemblyman Sullivan asked exactly how many more apartments the university needed. The answer was "around one thousand." Sullivan "could not understand why there was so much rancor and discord over 1000 extra units of housing," given that there are fifty to sixty thousand apartments between 106th and 125th streets. He blamed Columbia's "enclave mentality" and its "need and desire to control everything." Once again he suggested that Columbia replace dilapidated and abandoned housing in adjoining neighborhoods with mixed housing for local and university people, or that it rent apartments elsewhere in Manhattan and sublet them to affiliates.

These optimistic measures would require not only state funding, difficult to obtain, but an unprecedented flexibility on Columbia's part, a willingness to entertain seriously the notion of mixed housing and to relinquish its vision of the kind of insular, centripetal ambience offered by universities such as Yale or Princeton. (Accessories include the high-priced boutiques, ice cream parlors, and gourmet delicatessens lately springing up on the ground floors of university-owned buildings, replacing smaller, less toney stores in a process of gentrification gripping the city at large.) Such flexibility would, moreover, be in direct contradiction to the advice of the Senate panel's Final Report:

> The University would be in a strong position, especially if it gained control of its stock and tightened its control over the allocation of

desirable apartments, to improve its competitive position in what has been and will remain an increasingly competitive academic market.

In this setting, it is plain to see how a fire in 547 Riverside Drive, a "Gold Coast" location housing a dozen tenants who would most likely cleave—legally—to their rent-controlled apartments till death, might be construed by the university as an opportunity very hard to resist.

6 Our Town

During the limbo-like period in March, when the university's response to inquiries about the building was "I'll let you know," the tenants met every Thursday evening in Assemblyman Ed Sullivan's office, ten blocks south of 547. Kenny Schaeffer, Sullivan's legal aide, who devotes at least half his time to representing tenants involved in housing disputes with Columbia, advised them on possible courses of action. (Sullivan and Frank Barbero of Brooklyn are the only assemblymen in New York State who employ a full-time lawyer handling primarily tenant problems.) Afterwards they would go out for rowdy dinners in a local Chinese restaurant, which buoyed their spirits. At one such dinner they indulged in the fantasy of being rich enough to buy a co-op building together.

They also tried to keep the issue in the forefront of the Columbia community through local publicity, mainly in the *Spectator,* and circulated leaflets asking neighbors for their support: "If you are living in a Columbia building, this could happen to you, too." Harry called the Mayor's Action Office, which arranged for coverage on Channel 5; a reporter interviewed Inge Irving and Jerry and Selma Silverstein about the loss of their homes, and the clip ran on the evening news. Jerry called the *Daily News* and the

New York Post, asking them to follow up their stories of the fire with coverage of its aftermath.

"At the same time," Harry says, "I was making calls back to the local political leaders, asking them to write and call the university about our two points: temporary housing and rebuilding. They were uniformly on our side, though not too surprised. They were accustomed to Columbia ousting people from apartments, but this was something unique—benefiting from a fire to gain housing. Of course, in something like this, politicians can score points easily, since Columbia is not too popular locally. They can say, Look, these people ousted by the fire are not getting any help. And the university plays right into their hands, meanwhile complaining that it gets a bad press."

Through his professional work, Harry had been familiar for twenty years with the dynamics of neighborhood groups in conflict with institutions and government authority. He had been a city planner, first at Mobilization for Youth, a social service agency on New York's Lower East Side, and then in his own consulting firm. He says he persisted in this struggle because he thought it had to be done. "People were suffering—I felt a great responsibility. In the past I've helped groups to organize and suggested strategies and political contacts for getting things they wanted. My general outlook, professionally, has been helping people who need help or who are suffering or denied things. And here we were being treated as a kind of less deserving class.

"We all, including the politicians, felt Columbia had different responsibilities than ordinary landlords because it owned so much of the housing in the neighborhood and because it had profited not only by public money but also by favorable court decisions that gave it much more control over apartments than any private landlord has. Columbia has enjoyed this preferential treatment precisely because it's an educational institution. And yet the Columbia people always say, Why do you expect more from us than from a private landlord? When it's to their benefit, they want to be just another landlord. And when they're seeking special treatment in court, they want to distinguish themselves through their educational purpose. Depending on the situation, they play both sides of the street."

Possibly in response to political pressure, in the latter half of March Columbia offered to house the tenants of 547 in hotels at the rate of $75 a day. The tenants were stunned by this figure, which amounted to several times the monthly rent of a Morningside Heights apartment. Joan Regelin's reaction was: "Terrific. I asked whether I might have the money instead." The answer was no. Most drew the inference expressed by a community leader: "The fact that the university was willing to spend enormous amounts of money to relocate them downtown was an indication Columbia wanted them out of the neighborhood." It was feared that with the tenants out of sight, the university would consider itself discharged of obligations and free to rebuild for its own purposes. Nevertheless, since housing in Manhattan is scarce even at wildly inflated prices, a number of tenants were interested, until they discovered an accompanying document to be signed:

> I hereby request Columbia University to reimburse me for the sum of ______ representing one month's charges for space to be occupied at the ______ Hotel. I will pay the hotel directly.
>
> I understand and agree that Columbia is not legally obliged to reimburse me. I further agree that the University will not be required and will not reimburse me for any other sum in excess of that indicated above. Any other hotel or related charges incurred during that one-month period will be borne by me. I agree that all charges of any kind beyond the one-month period will be borne by me.

This would mean laying out several thousand dollars—far more than any of us would or could normally have allotted for monthly rent—with no written assurance of being reimbursed. In general, in the words of Inge Irving, the document "did not inspire confidence." Vice-President Gregory Fusco eventually conceded that it was "poorly drafted and was ambiguous on its face," and wondered if it might be "repaired." Meanwhile none of the tenants accepted the offer.

The problem of 547 Riverside Drive was on the agenda of the March 22 meeting of the Advisory Board on Residential Housing Policies and Management, held in the usual dark-hued conference room in The Riverside Church. Claude Morton, Columbia's new vice-president for investments, announced to local leaders that the engineers' preliminary findings on the building would not be made public, only the "final report," when it was complete. But the final report, Kenny Schaeffer protested, "would take shape in conformity with the University's interests. . . . The elected officials would feel more at ease if they could see the engineers' reports as they come in." This the university refused to permit.

Because of its refusal, along with the accumulation of other unpromising conditions—the chained doors, the waivers to be signed, the absence of any visible repairs, especially to the open roof—the tenants acknowledged with reluctance that Columbia evidently would not voluntarily restore the damaged apartments but instead hoped to use the building for its own purposes. "They were putting us off in increments," Rebecca Rikleen said. "We felt led on, then baffled, given the green light, then a roadblock, and never realizing we were headed for nowhere. Finally we understood." Kenny Schaeffer outlined what the legal remedies were; the most suitable was called a Housing Preservation (HP) Action. The group asked him to draw up the necessary papers. "I never really felt it was an out-and-out battle at the time," Rebecca went on. "I felt it was to get things moving a little bit." The issue in the Housing Preservation suit would be whether Columbia was obliged to rebuild.

The first legal step, on March 23, was to obtain a temporary restraining order (TRO) barring Columbia from demolishing the building and ordering it to restore utilities and allow south-wing tenants to return home. This was quickly accomplished by submitting papers stating the building was in violation of the Housing Code and in danger of being demolished, to the detriment of the imminent Housing Preservation suit. The TRO was short-lived, though. Columbia attorneys succeeded in having it overturned, or "vacated," the following day, by offering an affidavit vividly describing the condition of the building and claiming that the TRO had been granted only because "this Court was not fairly presented with the facts. . . . Petitioners would have this Court believe that the damages to the building were so insignificant that all that the landlord has to do is to switch on the electricity and oil burner and the building is ready for occupancy."

Damages to the building were certainly not insignificant. With the way it looked, smelled, and felt on March 23, it was inconceivable that anyone could have wished to live in it the next day. I asked Kenny Schaeffer if he was serious when he told a *Spectator* reporter, after obtaining the TRO, that there was a "definite possibility" of some tenants moving back in. Yes, he replied, the TRO was not merely a gesture of bravado; he could envision certain tenants moving back in if the utilities were turned on. Besides the question of principle, having the building occupied would improve the chances of prevailing in the Housing Preservation Action.

Kenny is an extremely keen and unreadable man who at thirty-three had already spent five years defending tenants' rights on

Morningside Heights; his manners are impersonal and his convictions passionate. From the time he was a child, he says, he wanted to be a public interest lawyer. "In law school I considered other fields—environmental law, labor law. Tenant law seemed the most immediate way to get engaged—that was what we called it in those days: engaged. There were millions of people and so much raw material to work with, and a lot of need. Private tenant lawyers were very expensive and not always available to moderate- and low-income people. Once I saw the special rules operating with Columbia, I became an expert in those situations. In fact, someone recently told me I was the only one in the city doing affiliation cases. I find it interesting, working with the community, trying to help people against large institutions and corporations. The legal problems involved are interesting too." He shrugs at being reminded that most young lawyers just out of school are after the $50,000-a-year jobs. "I was willing to work for the wages here. I wasn't looking to get rich from it. Those people are of two kinds—the kind who went to law school in order to get rich, and the kind who don't know what they want to do or why they went. I knew why I was going to law school. My influences were Eugene Debs and Clarence Darrow."

And so, I asked again, did you really think some tenants would move back in? After a pause, he said, "If they decided not to, given the inconveniences, that should be by their own choice."

That is to say, the issue was less whether a dozen or so families would return to a foul-smelling, dank building, and more whether a powerful institution was above obeying the law, which had already declared such conditions in violation of the Housing Code. Columbia had received and ignored two Buildings Department violations, on March 3 for the north wing and on March 21 for the south wing, both answerable in Criminal Court. Moreover, the vacate order itself has a dual purpose: along with forbidding occupancy goes the order for the landlord to make the building habitable once more. Yet by the end of March the promised engineers' reports were still not forthcoming, nor was any indication of the university's plans, other than Vice-President Fusco's statement that "the most likely scenario is that we will get some indication of the restorability of the building and then try to restore it."

On March 25, the day after the TRO was vacated, the Columbia University Senate met; on its agenda was a discussion of the specially appointed panel's Final Report on housing and rental policy. Kenny Schaeffer attended the meeting at the request of a member of the Senate staff who expected that the matter of 547 would be considered. But first Kenny leafletted outside with a one-page statement on behalf of the tenants, asking that the university "resist whatever temptation it may feel to resolve its own perceived housing shortage by taking advantage of the fire in any way." According to Kenny, at the Senate meeting a student asked university president Michael Sovern, "What are you going to do for the tenants of 547?" He replied, "Well, the tenants went to court and got a court order, but my understanding is that we got that vacated, isn't that so, Mason?" Mason Harding, university counsel, said, "Yes." So ended the Senate discussion of a building which the university had owned and managed for sixteen years.

The tenants filed their Housing Preservation suit during the last week in March, formally seeking an order to have Columbia restore 547 to its original condition. At Kenny's urging, because this would be a precedent-setting case with considerable financial stakes for both sides, they hired a prominent tenant lawyer, Len Lerner, as co-counsel. He had an excellent reputation, his fees were low, he answered his own phone and returned calls (unlike other attorneys being interviewed by Joan Regelin and Jerry Silverstein), and he was willing to act in an advisory or on-call capacity and allow Kenny to handle most of the courtroom and leg work. Lerner recommended an engineer who could evaluate the state of the building and give expert testimony. To their satisfaction, the tenants were joined in the suit by New York City's Housing Preservation Department (HPD), represented by Irwin Wiederkehr, who proved to be an advocate of unusual clarity and astuteness.

After the HP papers were served, but a few days before the trial officially began, the university unexpectedly sought a meeting with the tenants. "I had been sending Dais my little memos," recalls Harry, "and kept bombarding him with phone calls. Finally the court case galvanized it. He called and said, Let's meet."

The practical arrangements were impeded by mutual mistrust. The Columbia men refused to meet in 547 or in Ed Sullivan's office—they were miffed at Kenny's filing suit, calling it a "violation of protocol." The tenants refused to meet in university offices. At the last minute, the neutral territory of International House, several buildings south of 547, was agreed upon. Columbia refused to allow any political representatives or members of the press to attend.

In addition to Larry Dais and Daniel Rosenblatt, a new face from the university appeared: John Moriarty, director of real-estate investments, who worked under Vice-President Claude Morton. Moriarty's presence apparently brought a breath of optimism. Tenants saw him as "smooth," "suave," "reserved"; at the very least, he was new and relatively untainted by the accumulated suspicion and hostility; above all, he "seemed to be in charge."

Moriarty began by expressing surprise and a sense of injury that the tenants—ill-advised by Kenny—would choose court rather than trust Columbia to respond humanely to their requests. He then proceeded to the bad news: almost a month after the fire, the long-awaited engineers' final reports were still not ready, and thus no decision about the restoration could be announced. (Or as Dais was quoted in the next day's *Spectator,* "There's still a lot of uncertainty relative to its structure and relative to when we could begin repairs.") The sixth-floor parapet on the north side and part of the brick wall below were still in danger of collapse, and no one knew yet how much gas might be stored in the pipes or how damaged the plumbing and electrical systems might be. When Harry questioned why this was still so "after four agonizing weeks," the response was that work had been delayed by the March 23 TRO, in effect for one day.

The encouraging news was, first, the renewed offer of hotel stays, this time without the signing of any waiver. Second, and more important, Columbia now offered the tenants temporary or permanent housing in nearby buildings—a complete reversal of policy. "Sort out your poorest and most needy," the group was told, and they would be served first (an approach Kenny interpreted as "divide and conquer"). The apartments offered would be comparable to those in 547, though most likely not on Riverside Drive; the rents would be at the rates charged affiliates—substantially higher than the tenants' rent-controlled levels, yet lower than those on the city's open market. The tenants would not forfeit any other of their rent-control rights by accepting either the hotel or temporary housing, nor their right to return to 547 should it eventually be restored. None of these stipulations would be put in writing, though, on the grounds that legal documents had best be avoided. (Or as one tenant's notes have it, "CU: You didn't want to sign things so we don't.") Meanwhile, security guards would remain at the building and the university would help tenants move out their furniture and possessions.

The question on everyone's mind was finally asked: Are you

planning to break up the units for students? No, was the answer; we're waiting for the engineers' reports. The tenants then suggested a conciliatory plan of their own. Would the university be willing to have all twelve tenants resettle permanently in the south, and less damaged, wing, thereby keeping the north wing for its own purposes but leaving none homeless? (The south wing, where five of the tenants already lived, contained twelve apartments; counting a few previously vacant, as well as several formerly housing Columbia affiliates, it could readily accommodate those who would cross the hall from the north wing.) Anything is possible, came the response.

The offer of temporary housing or a month—prepaid—at a hotel was a practical relief for Jerry and Selma Silverstein, who had been living in Jonathan Irving's apartment while he was away. They immediately moved into the Hotel Esplanade, a large and quite handsome building about two miles south, a block from Riverside Park. Despite the Esplanade's air of faintly decaying gentility, its rooms were comfortable and spacious, and the surrounding neighborhood more lively, colorful, and safe than Morningside Heights. Rebecca and Ethan Rikleen left their sleeping bags on the floor of the day care center to stay at the Esplanade as well: "This was like a palace compared to The Red Balloon. We had some privacy, we had some space, we had a change of scene. There you were always hiding your things."

Despite the commute from her friends' home in New Jersey, Joan Regelin "panicked" at the idea of life in a hotel room. "I imagined we would be cramped, it would be a terrible existence. I thought, I can't, I just can't do it. I can't make myself make another move like that. At the house we had meals at regular times, I had pots and pans to cook in. Even more, the support and help of our friends was invaluable to us. I thought, How will I manage with the five of us in one room, with a hot plate?"

Likewise, Harold Lurier felt that his mother would not want to stay in a hotel; he wrote to John Moriarty asking for the money instead, which he could use to house Mrs. Lurier, but Moriarty never answered his letter. Mrs. Lurier remained at her other son's house in Buffalo while Harold tried, with no success, to find her a suitable apartment through the Columbia Housing Office. He was hoping for a place on the same block as 547, but none of the tenants who visited the Housing Office in April, in response to Moriarty's offer, were shown apartments on Riverside Drive. All of the apartments offered were in the real-estate category called "other."

One young tenant was given an apartment on West 112th Street, some ten blocks south of 547, while an older woman was offered a small walk-up apartment on a side street some five blocks from 547. Although she found it tiring to climb stairs, she accepted it out of need, and because a representative of the Housing Office told her she would have to remain there only about four months, which she took to mean that 547 would be rebuilt by then. "I lug the shopping cart up the stairs," she remarked later, "and when I get up there I have to sit down for half an hour. I don't feel up to par and haven't since the fire. If you can't live in your surroundings, if you don't know where your clothing is . . ."

Diana Angel was shown apartments on West 115th Street and West 112th Street, but she refused to go farther than where Adrienne was. This block, she asserted, was her home, her place. She also wanted to be near Adrienne for the sake of her health. Finally, about two and a half months after the fire, Columbia offered Diana a two-room apartment in 530 Riverside Drive, Adrienne's building, at the same rent she paid in 547, most of it covered, as before, by a city subsidy granted partly because of her age and partly for her disability. She furnished the apartment with donations from friends and purchases from the Volunteers of America and the Salvation Army Store, since all she had salvaged from her old apartment were some silver and a few sets of shelves.

Inge Irving had no time in early April to visit the Housing Office and look at apartments. As a travel agent, she was in the midst of her most hectic season, made even more busy because she was running the business alone now: her sister Eva had died of cancer the year before. Inge still clung to the hope that the building would be repaired, perhaps by the end of the summer. Just before the fire, she had had her apartment painted and the carpets cleaned; she had also finished cleaning up Eva's apartment and disposing of her things; with a sense of relief and accomplishment, she had felt her apartment was "all set to go." Moreover, she was irked at the kind of housing being offered. "The university thinks so little of its tenants and students, the only housing shown to us was 'student housing.' There is this class distinction between housing for different groups that has no place in the twentieth century."

Although the concession of temporary shelter was generally welcomed, the future of the building was as uncertain as before. And the tenants saw no reason, legal or otherwise, why their return home should be endlessly delayed, given that only four apartments out of the twenty-four needed massive work done. "It was a homestead," Rebecca says. "It seems silly to say that about a rented apartment, but it was. For a transient neighborhood—students, faculty, immigrants—there were a number of people with deep roots, long-term residents. It was a pleasant neighborhood where you could grow up and spend your life. There was the park, decent neighbors, space and air. It was a part of my life, my marriage, my children. Riverside Park was part of it, Cherry Park was part of it, International House, Riverside Church, the river, even the meat processors down by the pier. It was our town, that immediate neighborhood."

And so, in the end, the tenants accepted the inducements without yielding on the main issue. April Fool's Day would see them in court.

7 In Court

The Housing Part of New York Civil Court, a local court of limited jurisdiction, was set up in 1973 to enforce the city's Housing Maintenance Code and the New York State Multiple Dwelling Law, which sets standards of housing for cities of over 325,000 people. Both these laws cover cases of disrepair or failure to meet standards, but do not concern themselves with what may have caused the disrepair or violation. The Housing Part contains several trial "parts," each with its own judge. In 1983, Judge Harriet George presided over Part D, which handled cases of tenants seeking repairs from a landlord. Technically, in such cases the tenants are also suing the city to uphold and enforce the law, but often in practice the city (in this instance the Housing Preservation Department) joins in on the side of the tenants. According to Kenny Schaeffer, "There were other judges in other parts who were considered more liberal than Judge George. However, I felt she would be fair for the case: she is a family-oriented person, conservative, decent, and not a coward. She would not be intimidated by Columbia University." Len Lerner, the tenants' co-counsel, had appeared often before Judge George in his extensive practice as a tenant lawyer. He found her "good in the Housing Part. She likes to enforce.

She's an enforcer. So let her enforce against landlords rather than against tenants."

The case opened with Kenny Schaeffer's describing the effects of the fire: "a fair amount of damage to several of the apartments in the north wing and a fair amount of water damage to the rest of the north wing, and . . . very little damage whatsoever to the south wing." He asked for an order that Columbia correct the damage, based on the jurisdiction of the Housing Part and on the March 3 vacate order; he also requested that the utilities in the south wing be restored as soon as possible so that those tenants could return to their homes.

In response, Columbia's attorney called the building "destroyed by fire." As a result, he continued, "the relation of landlord and tenants was terminated and the owner was under no obligation to reconstruct for the benefit of former statutory tenants. . . . This proceeding has no basis in law." Finally, Irwin Wiederkehr, attorney for the Housing Preservation Department, in effect arguing on behalf of the tenants, pointed out that according to the recently amended Administrative Code, a vacate order is now "an order to repair. . . . Repairs are eminently feasible in this case," Wiederkehr went on, "and I believe that the respondent, Columbia University, is seeking to convert this into a windfall for them in order to take this building off the rental market." Thus the main lines of the case were drawn.

For the remainder of the trial, "Time Is on My Side" might have been the university's theme song; weather, too. The unusually heavy March rains had greatly increased water damage on the north, and still roofless, side of the building. Delay was the refrain, with a persistent trill of motions by Columbia seeking to have the case dismissed on a variety of grounds. At the outset, Columbia's attorney, Byron Golden, moved for an adjournment on the grounds that Ronald Golden, Columbia's registered managing agent for the building (no relation to the attorney), could not be present in court.

> Ronald Golden is of the Catholic faith and is observing today as Good Friday. His attendance is impossible because of the practice of his religion. . . . Due process demands that a defendant have the right to be present and that if the reason for his inability to be present is the practice of his religion, that my client would be deprived of his constitutional rights if this proceeding were to go on today. I therefore request a short adjournment, perhaps until Wednesday of next week. . . .
>
> MR. SCHAEFFER: First of all, today is not a legal holiday. It is a business day for the Court. My clients have been greatly prejudiced by the events of the last 30 days. Secondly, part of this case was on yesterday. . . . At the landlord's request the case was adjourned from yesterday until today and no request was made in court that it not be today and no information was given that they would not be ready to go ahead today.
>
> I assume if Mr. Golden is a Catholic today, he was a Catholic yesterday, and if this information was known to Mr. Golden, the attorney, this is a delaying tactic. . . .
>
> THE COURT: . . . I think we have put a lot of time and effort into this and . . . we are going to go ahead. I have every respect for everyone's religion, and I note here several people in this courtroom have asked to be excused by one o'clock so that they can go and attend Good Friday services, which are normally in the afternoon and in the evening. I myself am not observing today, but when it is my day to observe Holy Friday, that is the time I will go to church. So, I think he could have been here in the morning and gotten this thing over with.
>
> He didn't appear yesterday and he didn't make this motion yesterday. He didn't make it before me this morning initially off the record, and now he is making it on the record. I think it has to be looked at, in light of everything, as a little bit skeptical, and for that reason, I am denying the motion to adjourn. . . .
>
> MR. GOLDEN: May I respectfully request that your Honor confirm that which I witnessed in court shortly before this case was called?

> . . . The very same application was made for an adjournment on religious grounds, . . . and your Honor granted that application. I don't know why your Honor is differentiating between different practitioners of the same faith.
>
> THE COURT: For two reasons. One of which was, it was on for the first time here before me, and it was the first time it was made. The second reason is I didn't think it was of such urgency that would require it. . . . I have no knowledge about this case other than off the record I was told it is in danger of imminent collapse. I think without further ado, if there is such a tremendous interest in the health and safety of the people, let's get to the merits.
>
> MR. GOLDEN: May I indicate this is the first time this case is on before you.
>
> THE COURT: . . . It was on yesterday and they could have made that application yesterday. . . . You know, counselor, you are talking about Ronald Golden. I don't know who he is. I don't know what relationship he has here, but there are also trustees of Columbia University. I don't think Ronald Golden is responsible to hold up this building which you tell me is in imminent danger of collapse. Let's get on with it.

During the sixteen subsequent days of testimony, Ronald Golden rarely if ever availed himself of his constitutional right to be present in the courtroom, and according to the transcript, did not testify.

Byron Golden next requested the opportunity to submit a written motion that the case be dismissed on jurisdictional grounds; his position was that while the court could order repairs of conditions that violate the Housing Code, it had no such power in the case of a building which was "substantially demolished and . . . presently vacant." Ironically, the building was vacant precisely because Columbia had ignored the Buildings Department order to repair, and had not restored utility service to the south wing, which was not under a vacate order. This motion, too, was denied.

Before the petitioners formally presented their case, Irwin

Wiederkehr asked that the court enjoin the university from demolishing the building, or from doing anything that might make it impossible for the tenants to return, should they win the case. "The way things stand now," Wiederkehr said, "the trustees of Columbia University could go in and totally demolish the building." Indeed, workmen on the premises and engineers bearing blueprints had fed, rightly or not, this suspicion that the case might overnight be left without a corpus. The judge responded:

> I want them to continue to make repairs only to the extent of safeguarding the area. I don't want them to further demolish or to go on or do anything else extensive. As far as putting up a temporary roof, I see no problem with that, and I will allow them to do that. They may not do anything else . . . until the disposition of this matter is taken care of.

Kenny Schaeffer tried to press the judge to order Columbia to comply with the vacate order and repair the building, but of course that would have been virtually deciding the case in advance. "I have to decide whether or not they are going to do that," she said rather sharply. "That is why I am here. That is why we are hearing this."

The petitioners' case, conducted by Kenny Schaeffer and Len Lerner, was two-pronged: testimony by Richard Balser, a civil engineer, on the structural condition of the building and the extent of the needed repairs, and testimony by the tenants describing their apartments before and after the fire. Balser, a remarkably unflappable witness, was questioned strenuously by both sides over a period of two days. Despite Byron Golden's attempts to embarrass him by demonstrating that he could not quote from the Administrative Code and that he was paid for time spent giving expert testimony (common practice among professionals), the engineer kept doggedly to the findings of his inspection: that the building could certainly be repaired and was not in "imminent danger of collapse" except for part of the roof masonry on the north side, which would not affect the south side; that most apartments in the south wing would be habitable but for the lack of utilities ("The 'B' line lower floor apartments, for example, 2B, has got a kind of water damage I would characterize as equivalent to damage from an overflowing bathtub"); that checking of the gas and electrical lines, fixing part of the roof, "drying out," plastering and painting the south wing could be accomplished in about a month; that the north wing, requiring extensive work, could be restored in six to nine months; that the total cost of restoration would be about $1 million as compared to $5 million to demolish and construct a new building.

At the end of the first day of testimony, Judge George announced, "I intend to go there on Monday with my inspectors."

> MR. SCHAEFFER: They are coming Tuesday.
>
> THE COURT: I am going Monday. Whoever wants to go Tuesday, that is their department. You will be here on Wednesday morning to continue the trial. The conditions that existed on March 2 you have all known about. You have to give the Court a chance to look at it.

"Do you want counsel present on Monday?" Byron Golden inquired. "It is not necessary," the judge replied. "I would prefer that nobody be there except somebody to open the facilities and let us in."

When the trial resumed two days after the judge's trip to the building, Byron Golden protested "grave improprieties."

> I would like the record to reflect that prior to the time this trial commenced last Friday, a gentleman who identified himself as being from the Borough President's Office of the Borough of Manhattan came before this Court, addressed this Court and said words to the

effect—and I do not wish to imply that I'm giving it verbatim—the gist of it was, "I want the Court to know that the Borough President is very interested in this case"; . . . I have reason to believe that that representative was asked to come to Court by counsel, specifically Kenneth Schaeffer.

I respectfully submit, your Honor, that that kind of blatant attempt to improperly influence this Court is a very serious matter and I would, with your Honor's permission, like to ask Mr. Schaeffer that [*sic*] he caused that representative from the Borough President's office to come to Court last Friday and attempt to influence the Judge's judgment of this Court.

MR. SCHAEFFER: Would you like me to respond? No, I did not. The Borough President's Office has been interested in this affair since the day it occurred or the day afterward. They, as I understand it, they feel that it's important as preservation of housing stock, that the relief requested be granted. And they came of their own free will, and that I have no control of the Office of the Borough President of Manhattan. . . .

MR. GOLDEN: You were unaware that they were coming?

MR. SCHAEFFER: I didn't say I was unaware. I just said I did not ask them. They told me they were coming.

MR. GOLDEN: Did you or someone on behalf of the—

MR. SCHAEFFER: Excuse me; is this an interrogation, your Honor? I object.

THE COURT: I'm going to call him to this because I heard the gentleman and all he did was say, "I would like to make a statement. I'm from the Borough President's Office," and . . . they indicated to him, from the other side of the table, they preferred he didn't make any statement. At that time he walked out. Now what else are we going to make about this?

MR. GOLDEN: Your Honor—

THE COURT: If you're afraid that those words "Borough President" had anything to do, you know, with my feelings or anything about this case, just disabuse yourself of that, sir. I don't know the Borough President of Manhattan. I've never met him and I may never meet him. I have nothing to do with him. He has nothing to do with me.

MR. GOLDEN: Your Honor—

THE COURT: Okay. I don't care about it so let's just go ahead. Just don't worry about that if that's on your mind.

The next "grave impropriety" to which Golden objected was that despite the judge's preference that nobody accompany her on her tour of the building, Kenny Schaeffer did so. (Several tenants trailed along as well, entering their own and their friends' apartments.)

THE COURT: Tell me something, Mr. Golden. Who is that gentleman over there?

MR. GOLDEN: He is an employee of Columbia University.

THE COURT: He never left my side, okay? Right, Mr. Gorman?

MR. GORMAN: Yes, your Honor.

THE COURT: You introduced yourself and you were kind enough to give me a flashlight and you accompanied me the entire time and you helped me on several occasions. I didn't even know who you were or where you were from. You looked like a gentleman, and when you helped me over some dangerous places, I appreciated it. Now let's get this: True, . . . I always prefer that the fewer people the better because we're going into people's homes. In this case they were not occupied but usually they are and sometimes it's very intimidating to people. It also is a lot of noise to me. . . . Now he didn't give any testimony; he just took us places. . . . There was another tall gentleman . . . and when asked who he was, he said he worked for Columbia. So let's put this one to rest.

I've been through too many inspections to be influenced by anybody, be they attorneys, be they tenants, be they landlord. I go there with my inspector and I use my two eyes and I look. That's why I went, because I want to see the topographical layout of that building . . . and where the fire was so that when you come here and talk to me, you have, so to speak, a hot court, okay?

Now, if your feeling is you want to ask me to recuse myself, I'm not going to do it.

Golden continued to object until the judge called the discussion a "waste of time . . . unless you want to make some sort of motion." He moved first that a hearing be held immediately "to determine exactly what took place on Monday," which was denied; second, for a mistrial, also denied; and lastly, "most reluctantly and respectfully," that the judge recuse herself (that is, withdraw from the case).

> THE COURT: All right, the only way I can recuse myself is if I was related in any degree financially or by blood or I felt that I could not fairly hear this case. And as I'm fond of saying, it would give me great pleasure to recuse myself . . . and get on with all these cases, but being brought up in the work ethic that I was, I couldn't honestly tell you that I've been in any way tainted by my visit there to the extent that I would have to send this case back. I would be lying. I took the time to go so justice wouldn't be blind. Okay?

The recurring motif in the tenants' testimony, which followed that of Richard Balser, was their wandering in and out of each other's variously damaged homes—something their lawyers had suggested in order to get eyewitness testimony on every apartment. Inge Irving testified that her apartment was in the same condition in the first week of April as before the fire, and that Rebecca Rikleen's was too. "Had you been in that apartment before the fire?" Len Lerner asked. "Many times." She also testified about the condition of 6A: "Mr. Schwartz is out of town and he wanted me to, you know, just say what I saw." In addition, she had visited 4B, the apartment next door to her own, and found it undamaged.

Joan Regelin testified that the condition of her apartment on April 6 was "very bad" compared to the day after the fire. Plaster from the ceilings had fallen in almost every room, because of the continuing rain.

> Q. [KENNY SCHAEFFER]: Can you explain why you think rain could have come into your apartment?

A. Well, there has been no roof or any protective covering on the building whatsoever since the day of the fire. . . . I went up to the top of the building to see what the situation actually was. . . . Every time it rains it rains directly into the building, increasing the damage . . . on the north.

She also testified to walking through 6A, 6C, and 6D.

Another tenant, Yvonne Uehling, corroborated that in her first-floor apartment, below Joan's, initially little damaged on March 3, "the water is getting heavier, the moldings on the walls are coming out and, and everything is just a lot wetter so the plaster is falling down." She added that she had also examined apartments 5D, 4D, and 4C.

Harold Lurier testified about the conditions of his mother's and aunt's apartments, as well as of the Maggarts', next door, "and I have been in Mrs. Irving's apartment for the tenant meetings." Harold's aunt, Diana Angel Stamoulis, succeeded him on the witness stand.

Q. What was the condition of your apartment prior to the fire on March 2nd?

A. Very beautiful. . . .

Q. Have you been in the apartment since the fire?

A. Yes.

Q. When was the last time?

A. The last time that I have been inside the apartment was March 5th but I have been walked up to the door, only emotionally when I saw the blackness I could not go in. The first eight days I was very ill. I could not go near the apartment at all.

Q. When you went in the apartment on March 5th and when you have observed it since then from the doorway, what was the condition of the apartment on March 5th?

A. On March 5th it was in the condition of total destruction, that is the word. I wouldn't take you through all the details.

Q. Mrs. Stamoulis, do you want to have the apartment restored?

A. Yes. I have lived in that apartment all my life, practically, adult life. I moved into New York when I was very young.

Q. How long have you lived in this particular apartment?

A. Since early 1958.

This frequent coming and going sprang from something more than the curiosity that disasters inspire, or the arrangements to testify on behalf of those who could not be present. Certainly Inge would look at 3A: Rebecca had been her downstairs neighbor ever since she moved in with Ben twenty-five years before. Certainly she would look at 4B, next door—it was a point of honor with her to know her neighbors, in this case a young couple affiliated with Columbia and given new housing shortly after the fire. Certainly Yvonne would look at 5D—she had probably spent hours in there playing with the older Maggart children fifteen years back. And so on—a nightmarish reenactment of the habits of decades.

On Friday, April 8, after Richard Balser's statement that repairs could cost $1 million, Kenny Schaeffer and Irwin Wiederkehr served the respondents with subpoenas ordering them to produce two items: first, any pertinent architects', contractors', or engineers' reports in their possession, and second, documents regarding the university's insurance policies for 547 Riverside Drive. Columbia had had many experts examine the building, without divulging their findings or recommendations. Kenny believed these reports would support the tenants' contention that the building was eminently restorable. As for the insurance records, Kenny feared that Columbia would attempt to use cost as an argument in its defense, that is, claim that the cost of restoring the building made it a highly impractical undertaking. In several of the cases Columbia was citing as precedents, landlords had prevailed because the cost of repairs was judged to be "confiscatory." The insurance records would show that the university was fully covered for all repairs.

The need for the insurance records at this point in the trial, Kenny explains, arose from Columbia's not having returned a formal "answer" to the petitioners' suit at the start. In any lawsuit, the original petition states the cause of legal action, after which the respondents generally give an answer before the trial begins. Then the petitioners, aware of what the defense will consist of, can present their case accordingly. But if, as in this instance, no answer is offered to begin with, the petitioners are left rather in the dark about the line of defense. "In effect," Kenny says, "Columbia had no answer. Cost was their real answer, which kept coming up indirectly while the Housing Preservation Department and the tenants were putting on their case. And yet they didn't want to use cost directly as an affirmative defense because it was obvious they had the money to rebuild." The subpoena of documents was an effort to be prepared to respond, should cost be raised during the defense, or to forestall its being raised at all.

On April 12, when Columbia had neither answered the subpoena nor submitted a motion to quash it, the opposing attorneys complained to Judge George, who did not seem to believe any documents were needed. Why even bring in insurance records? she said. "The cost stands alone, whether there's insurance or not. . . . I have to decide what's the cost, basically, and is it a reasonable cost." Then, assuming that it is "within the realm of possibility" and that Columbia in its defense makes no mention of its ability to pay, her decision would be independent of cost or insurance.

Byron Golden conceded that, insurance or not, the university could afford to restore the building. He made it clear that the issue for Columbia was not one of means but of will—in other words, whether the university would choose to spend its insurance money to repair the apartments of unaffiliated tenants.

Throughout the trial the issue of cost proved to be a stumbling block. Since Judge George had ruled it out as a legitimate defense, she might have silenced Columbia's attorneys every time they brought it up. As it happened, she silenced them only intermittently, and so cost played an ambiguous role, not openly acknowledged but pervasive.

After much heated discussion, Columbia did agree to produce a motion to quash the subpoenas. But before that step, the entire issue was suspended. Outside of court, perhaps impelled by similar feelings of impatience, frustration, and doubt as to the outcome of the trial, both sides were beginning to weigh the alternative of a negotiated settlement.

8 A Stick in the Heart

During that week of trial, which took place a month after the fire, Diana Angel's daughter Connie, who lived in Florida with her husband and two daughters, was preparing to come to New York to help her mother. At first Diana had told her not to come since she was doing all right with Adrienne, but Connie was hurt and said her mother was shutting her out of her life at this terrible time. Connie, her cousin Harold remembers, was "frantic" to come. At last Diana said, "All right, then, come. I'm not trying to shut you out of my life. We have no furniture, but I'll have an apartment soon and we'll do the best we can." Connie went shopping for some household articles to bring up to her mother. On the way home, her car was hit by a truck driven by a nineteen-year-old. The top of the car was taken off and Connie died instantly. When Adrienne got the call and told her, Diana couldn't believe it was true and thought she would go crazy. Adrienne said, "I'll be all alone if you fall apart."

Harold had been very close to his cousin and was stunned by her death. His own mother was in Buffalo at the time, and knowing her poor health, he didn't tell her about it until after the funeral, which he arranged. Diana went down to Pompano Beach to attend. "I could never even see her body in the coffin because it was so mangled. The whole complex where she lived turned out for the funeral. People were wonderful. So how are you going to take life? It's a schizo thing. Sometimes it seems that life isn't worth anything to anyone anymore. This fire, which didn't have to happen. And that boy who was driving the truck, weaving in and out of traffic, got his license suspended for two years."

Harry had returned to Iowa City when the legal machinery took over and the trial began. After a week our phone began to ring, and soon every morning he would pace the floor for an hour or so at a time in the bedroom of our rented house, talking to John Moriarty of Columbia's Office of Investments about the prospect of negotiations out of court. The bedroom, converted from a sun porch, was long and narrow and many-windowed; the telephone had a very long cord. He would walk up and down the length of the room, into the hall and back, phone in hand, sometimes pausing to gaze out at our neighbor's flowering dogwood tree. From downstairs I could hear him speaking in paragraphs, then there were long silences and footsteps. Some days the tone was cordial, other days wary and businesslike. After he hung up he would pace some more, and later on tell me what they had talked about.

"The phone calls from Moriarty," he says now, "were about getting the process started: will we meet, is there enough mutual interest in it, what would the terms of a settlement be? Then around the thirteenth he said his side was 'eager' to reach an agreement and get the job done quickly. Perhaps they were starting to realize they didn't have much of a case. Also, I imagine they were rather surprised we stuck together as we did and went to court. In most cases they're evicting individuals, or they take over an SRO where people are without any resources to fall back on. So they must have calculated that they wouldn't meet a lot of opposition. Plus the fact that we were just the kind of people they want to eliminate—rent-controlled tenants from before 1971. But as it turned out, we felt strongly, and we had the publicity, the legal case, the political help."

The tenants, if not eager, were at least willing to negotiate, because even a favorable court decision might turn out to be ambiguous. For example, the judge might order Columbia to fix only the south wing, leaving the future of the north wing indefinite. Or Columbia might appeal a decision as far as the State Court of Appeals if it wished, meanwhile leaving the building to stand empty and deteriorate. Finally, a number of people felt that if they were to stay on as tenants of Columbia, it was better to have an agreement than an imposed decision, in order to avoid lasting hostility. (A negotiated agreement is still enforceable by the court.) "I'd say we were pretty much in favor of negotiating," Harry recalls. "We never really took votes over anything. Probably Harold Lurier and Joan were against negotiating and for staying in court."

By April 16 Harry had drawn up a proposed agreement which he sent to Kenny Schaeffer for the other tenants to review, and to have translated into legal language. This original draft reiterated the university's offer to pay for thirty days in a hotel or provide temporary housing while the building was being restored. It also suggested, as an alternative, that some tenants might relinquish their legal rights to the apartments in 547 if they were given comparable housing nearby at similar rents and with the same rent-control protection. Or that some might relinquish their rights to an apartment altogether, for an unspecified cash settlement. But since almost everyone wanted to return to 547, the key point was that those living in the north wing would move across to the south, leaving Columbia half the building for its affiliates. The proposed agreement stipulated a maximum of five months for restoration of the south wing but gave no date for the north —Moriarty had refused to commit the university on that point. It did provide that Columbia would not divide the north-wing apartments into smaller units, and when assigning housing would give preference to families, whether graduate students, faculty, or staff: the tenants hoped to keep the building from turning into a dormitory. And once the agreement was signed, the tenants would withdraw their Housing Preservation suit.

For seven weeks, until early June, the document was passed back and forth, each side making changes and adjustments. Long and complex meetings were held, one at International House on April 18, the following day at Inge Irving's midtown office, a week later at Irwin Wiederkehr's Housing Preservation Department office, and then at John Moriarty's Columbia office in the Wall Street area—rather like a traveling dinner party, a course at each stop. Meetings, like summit conferences, give the feeling of progress; at the May 3 session of the Advisory Board on Residential Housing Policies and Management, held in Riverside Church, a mood of optimism and all-around self-congratulation prevailed. Board Chairman Tom Kappner, noting that agreement seemed near,

> affirmed that it was results like these that vindicated the two and a half years' worth of Advisory Board meetings. He did, however, wish to express serious reservations about one aspect of the agreement taking shape. Tom strongly objected to the possibility that Columbia might restore the north wing by altering the apartment lay-out to conform more to dormitory needs. It would be most unfortunate, he said, if Columbia used the tragedy of the fire to gain dormitory space. . . .
>
> Larry Dais pointed out that the University had moved way beyond what any other landlord would have been expected to do in a compa-

rable situation. He wished to underline this fact and stressed that it should be noted. Larry also wished to observe that legal maneuvers are often an impediment to arriving at agreements.

At the tenant meetings, still held every Thursday at Assemblyman Sullivan's office, the spirit of tenacity was turning fretful. Jerry Silverstein, who remained at the Esplanade during April and May (on insurance money after Columbia's offer of a month ran out), was optimistic and active in the negotiations, but at the same time was looking for an apartment "until I was nauseous from looking. During this terrible period Selma had her practice, which was a stable force in her life, but I was completely adrift. There were no beginnings in my life, only endings."

Nena O'Neill attended all the meetings, even though she wasn't sure she wanted to return to 547. But she felt "the meetings gave people the strength to carry on—we had been hit by such a blow. I looked forward to the Chinese dinners we had afterwards. These evenings really helped me, buoyed me up through the disorientation. Later, as people began to take up their lives again and go their ways, I was disappointed, I had a sense of the continuity being lost. But throughout I felt I owed something to the group, to give support and bolster its numbers. If I dropped out it would be one less person. So I stayed. Nobody dropped out."

Harold Lurier, too, attended every meeting, even though he would have chosen to stay in court. "We had strength then, while Columbia was off balance, not sure what their strategy would be. I would have preferred taking a hard line all along. I said so in the beginning. Inge got angry at me, Jerry thought I was crazy. I remember at a second International House meeting about negotiations, Irwin Wiederkehr said, 'I am duty bound to warn these tenants that they are not wise to enter into this,' and I agreed. Moriarty was very irritated at Wiederkehr's remark and said something snide to him, such as, 'Ah, we didn't need you here.' I was sure he was a snob. I never trusted him. And Wiederkehr, as it happened, was excellent, he really did yeoman service. He was interested in our welfare, he worked hard and did a lot of running. Anyway, I was in a minority, and once it was decided, I negotiated as best I could."

Harold's mother returned to New York in May. Since he had to go to Europe, he arranged for her to fly to Texas. "She had old friends there, Greek friends from the same town, who had been inviting her for years." After that, Mrs. Lurier visited friends in San Francisco and San Diego, before returning to her daughter's house in Washington.

Joan Regelin was gradually becoming "infuriated" at the negotiations: she had thought the tenants were winning the case and had a good deal of momentum on their side. During April and May, Joan and her family were still living in the New Jersey farmhouse; she was still commuting several times a day, and becoming more depressed. "One thing saved me: a small tour—one week—with the New York Vocal Arts Quartet in California. I was able to do this because of my friend, who took care of the children. We performed a series of concerts of classical and romantic vocal music." With the rains continuing and no roof on the north side of the building, she and Christian had moved what remained of their furniture and other possessions to that area of the living room they thought would be damaged last. Joan worried most about her piano, not only because it was essential to her work, but because of its sentimental value—it had belonged to her grandfather.

Earlier in the spring, Joan had inquired at the Housing Office about vacant apartments on Riverside Drive and been told by James Kyrimes that no such apartments existed. But she did see a large apartment on 111th Street, about twelve blocks south of 547. "Kyrimes wouldn't tell me how much the rent was. He said they'd have to see, he'd have to look into it. Well, this was during our so-called friendly relations with Moriarty. It was also a time when we were getting the most publicity and Columbia was trying to get this thing hushed up. I called Moriarty and said, I'd like to come and speak with you. He said, Okay, when would you like to come? When I went there I said I had come to talk about where I could store the piano. I also hoped we could get reimbursed for our expenses since the fire. Because even though we had not taken advantage of the hotel offer, we had paid our friends rent, there was money spent for food, transportation, and endless phone calls. Then I asked him what the rent would be for that apartment on 111th Street. He said, Would you take it on a permanent basis? I said, Well, I didn't know, and again asked the rent. He said, What would the rent have to be? What would you pay? How about fifty dollars a month, would you take it for that? I was bewildered. I said, Are you really offering me the apartment for fifty dollars a month?

"This was a very quiet meeting. Madison Avenue type. It was such an experience that when I came out of there I knew I could not trust them for anything, and could not trust him. I came to my own conclusions, that we were only cutting our throats if we dealt with them on an individual level. I could tell we were headed for bad times."

As the negotiations proceeded, Joan learned through Columbia's attorney that with the academic year ending and students moving out, the university was indeed willing to offer her family an apartment comparable to her spacious north-wing one, but in another building. She and Christian were willing to consider the offer but wanted to be sure it was written into any agreement. (Joan approached the dealings with Columbia more skeptically than some others possibly because only three years earlier, the university had attempted, vigorously but unsuccessfully, to evict her family.) "But when the issue of writing in the provision about our apartment came up at meetings," she recalls, "we began to be looked at by the other tenants as a special case. When in fact we had never wanted that. Len Lerner kept talking and confusing the matter, and the other tenants became very angry at us."

In the midst of the negotiations, Rebecca and Ethan Rikleen had to leave the Hotel Esplanade because the month at Columbia's expense was over. Rebecca had still not removed anything from her undamaged apartment: "I always thought, next week I'd know how to plan my life." Through a classmate of Ethan's, she was able to stay at an apartment on West Sixty-eighth Street. "We were fortunate. I also performed some services for them in exchange—house-sitting, watering the plants, some cleaning. It was a nice neighborhood, but I had a bad feeling about being there. We didn't really have any privacy. When friends of the owners came to the city from out of town they stayed at the apartment, and so we left. We were always carrying around our suitcases."

In the middle of May, as negotiations proceeded, a group of tenants went to see the Reverend William Sloane Coffin of The Riverside Church to ask him to use his influence in urging Columbia to rebuild 547. Coffin promised to get in touch with some professors at the law school who might intercede with President Sovern, and if this failed, to hold a press conference. Near the end of the meeting, noting wryly that he was having trouble restraining himself, Coffin asked if he might make a few "pastoral" remarks. He said that when he was being led off to jail for his outspokenness during the Vietnam war, he happened to meet in the halls of the Federal Judicial Building his old friend Ramsey

Clark, then U.S. attorney general. Coffin was probably being his congenial self, for Clark asked, What are you so happy about? You're going to jail. Coffin replied, Do you think I would let the federal government dictate my state of mind? His lesson was not to let your adversaries define how you see the world, and not to live by nurturing grievances. Coffin likened grievances to a garden, and said some people sustain themselves by tilling this garden. When they wake in the morning, before they even get out of bed, they start turning the soil over and over, brooding on who has done them wrong.

After the meeting and the pastoral remarks were over, Inge and I walked the three blocks north to 547. It was a gorgeous spring day, the light particularly sharp and radiant. We got Mrs. Flanagan, stationed in the lobby, to let us into the basement; we had brought flashlights. We wanted to hunt for things, Inge for Victor's bicycle, and I for a double-bed frame stored down there. The basement was pitch black, dank, and swampy. More than two months after the fire, it had not yet been cleaned up or drained. The debris that was once the tenants' possessions stood in filthy water remaining from the rains that had poured through the unsealed roof. We squished our way through the muck. I thought I spied the bed frame rotting in a corner, but I decided not to wade through shin-deep black water to get to it. As far as Inge could see, Victor's bicycle was gone. Nonetheless, Inge says that she was deeply affected by Coffin's lesson and months later still drew on it for strength.

She also says she was infuriated by the negotiations. "At the beginning, I felt you get more with honey than with vinegar, but as time went on we came to realize the honey didn't work. While we were negotiating with them, Moriarty wouldn't talk to me. It was insulting. He said, I'll speak with Harry Schwartz. Occasionally he would call me back, but said he'd only deal with Harry.

But I'm a person, a human being. Yes, Moriarty was the worst; with him there was the feeling of the old boys' club. He didn't think a woman is quite human."

Meanwhile, the meetings the tenants held on their own were becoming more noisy and exhausting, from the effort to reach a unified position. And as a result, Rebecca believes, Columbia found Harry "intractable because he insisted on bringing all their proposals back to the group and getting a consensus. They wanted him to make decisions on his own, but he wouldn't. They tried to make a private deal with Harry, or so rumor has it." (Harry says no private deal was ever proposed.) Another tenant claimed to have seen blueprints in the Columbia engineer's makeshift office in apartment 1A which showed 547 divided into small units on each side. But when this possibility was raised at a meeting, she recalls, "Everyone said, 'Oh no, they're not going to do that.' They wouldn't listen."

Several of the tenants said very little at these meetings. As one person put it, "There were a few vocal people who managed things. And then there are always a few who are never happy, who get agitated about everything. But of course the meetings are useful—it's how to get things done. Although if I were in your husband's shoes, I would have walked out, especially with the things certain people said. I saw him change color several times."

The major sticking point in the negotiations was a time limit for rebuilding the north wing: Columbia refused to name a date. And the tenants refused to agree to move back into a building of which one-half would remain in squalid disrepair for an unknown period. Co-counsel Len Lerner said, "How in the world could I agree to that? It might be the millennium."

Harry says he had a premonition of the outcome as early as April 19, at the meeting with the Columbia officials held in Inge's office. "It seemed that we started out closer to agreement than we ended up. I believe at that point we still hadn't even agreed on a date for completing the south wing, when Joan brought up the issue of payment for individual damages. We others had warned her not to raise this; we felt it would be counterproductive. But she couldn't contain herself. It complicated the situation. They were still very evasive at that point. It was never clear to us—maybe even to them—who was in charge of making decisions. They said, Can we go out to caucus for a moment? And when they came back I could see that their faces were changed. Well, at the time I thought we might have settled then if Joan hadn't insisted on pursuing her personal concerns, but on the other hand she was a tenant and she had a right to express her feelings. Now, with hindsight, I tend to think the real reason was simply that they didn't want to give a date for the north side. I don't think they knew yet what they wanted to do with it.

"Moriarty could not recognize that we had an interest in when the whole building would be fixed. Also, for Columbia it was a matter of pride. Moriarty felt we were trying to get too much, to dictate what Columbia should do, which was none of our business. But if one half remained dangerous, naturally it would affect us. He felt we should trust that they were acting in good faith, even though they wouldn't put anything in writing. But by then we weren't about to trust that much—there still wasn't even a temporary roof.

"So we began with high hopes, but things began to deteriorate early. We tried to negotiate for too long. Once we saw it wasn't going to work out, we should have gone back to court right away."

As negotiations deteriorated, Joan and Christian suspected that the offer of temporary housing might be withdrawn. Besides the fact that no one would tell them the actual rent, the apartment on 111th Street needed much renovating, while another one, on

115th Street, was ready to be occupied. On Kenny's advice, they decided to take it while it was still available, "because the handwriting was on the wall," Joan says. "We signed the lease on June 1, a week before the negotiations broke down. The apartment is smaller, cramped, but livable.

"If they had just given us apartments right away, as they did with their affiliates . . . They didn't get such great apartments, but they took them because they were desperate. We would have done it too. But from the beginning their reaction was to consider us nonpeople. I also felt, with both Moriarty and Kyrimes, that I suffered a kind of thing because of being a woman—they would deal with me in a certain way that they wouldn't have with Harry. I felt I had to go in there and be very charming and—you know."

At the next meeting of the Advisory Board, on June 7, attended as usual by Columbia and community representatives, the tone of sweet reason had gone flat: Vice-President Gregory Fusco said that matters had been "negotiated to death," and that he "did not feel it appropriate to be bound by a specific time schedule."

> Ed Ortiz [from Congressman Ted Weiss's office] speculated . . . that the University had not yet determined what it would do with the north wing and it was therefore stalling.
>
> Greg Fusco remarked that this sounds like a reasonable speculation. . . .
>
> Sadly, Tom [Kappner] said, if the 547 tenants had been attending these meetings regularly, they would have witnessed one example after another of Columbia's callousness and disregard for basic human decency.

Fusco's remark was the tenants' definite notice that negotiations were over; accordingly, they arranged to resume the interrupted Housing Preservation suit in court. (Moriarty, in retrospect, told a *Spectator* reporter, "The tenants really blew it on this one," the fault being "their fundamental mistrust of the University.")

On June 8, the day after that meeting, another fire broke out in the empty building. It began at ten-fifty in the morning in 6B, Nena O'Neill's south-wing apartment, across the hall from where the March 2 fire had started, and spread to the fifth floor and the roof before it was termed under control by the Fire Department an hour later. Fire Marshal Louis Garcia was quoted in the June 15 *Spectator:* "Someone poured some flammable liquid on the sixth floor. It will be definitely declared arson. The most conceivable scenario was that someone came over the roof." He called it "an amateur job. A professional would have burned the building down."

Our family was camped temporarily in a friend's apartment nearby, and so I was in the neighborhood that morning and heard the sirens. Like anyone who has been a fire victim, I had ears and nerves keenly attuned to sirens. But I assured myself it could not be: a coincidence not even worthy of a bad movie. At about four in the afternoon, Harry phoned. He had heard the news from Inge.

Our eighteen-year-old daughter, Rachel, and I rushed over to meet Harry at the building. Standing out in front was Mrs. Flanagan, with the super from next door and her daughter, all marveling at the perversity of fate, just as they had marveled at less dramatic events in days gone by. Only Tom Kelly was missing. The building looked about the same, draped in scaffolding but defiantly, if gloomily, standing. The fire marshal had ordered that no one enter, Mrs. Flanagan warned, but Harry intended to see what had become of our remaining things. Among the tenants Harry was noted for his equanimity under stress and provocation, but now he rose above that fine quality and rushed into the building past the phalanx of supers. Like a Greek chorus, Mrs. Flanagan and her friend wailed that he might be killed, which made Rachel rush in after him. I called her back and told her he would be fine, though I wasn't altogether sure. I was sure, though, that given his months of self-containment at God knows what cost, it would be wrong to stop him now. We spent only five tense minutes before he returned, reporting that the hole in our living room ceiling was a little bigger, the north wall and adjacent furniture a little blacker. Nena's apartment was more charred than before, but relatively, the sixth-floor damage this time was slight. (Mrs. Lurier's first-floor apartment, barely touched by the March 2 fire, suffered severe water damage in this one. Harold, telephoned again by his cousin Adrienne, stood outside with Jonathan Irving, watching it "come down like Niagara," and later found two inches of water on the kitchen floor. Likewise, Joan's piano and some other furniture, which Columbia workmen had recently moved upstairs to an empty and undamaged south-wing apartment, were damaged this time.)

Harry was concerned because the plywood planks covering our gaping windows since March had been smashed by the firemen, leaving the apartment open on three sides, but Mrs. Flanagan did not have any remedy in mind. So we left the supers, who seemed nonplussed at Harry's emerging intact, and walked to the Columbia Housing Office seven blocks away, where Harry demanded to see the director, Daniel Rosenblatt. Word came back through the receptionist that he would not see us, nor would the assistant director, James Kyrimes. Harry's response (which till then, Rachel said, she had thought occurred only in movies and on TV) was to march past the receptionist, shouting, "He may not want to see us, but we want to see him!" Highly impressed, we marched after him, hunting for Rosenblatt in the warren of clean little white offices with walls that didn't reach the ceiling. Rachel spied him leaving from a side door, attaché case in hand. Harry accosted him, saying, "There's been another fire! What do you intend to do about it this time!" Rosenblatt turned his massive back on us, muttering, "I have to go to a meeting. This is not my responsibility." Rachel said later that she could not believe one person could behave that way to another. It may have been from that moment that I started treating her as an adult.

Finally we found John Chandler, to whom for many years we had relayed messages about dripping taps and the broken elevator, when complaints to Mrs. Flanagan were ineffectual. As area manager, he had been polite and behaved decently to the tenants. For a while Chandler and his family had lived next door in 548; our younger daughter and his had gone to school together, and on cold mornings he would drive them both. Now he explained regretfully that since March 18 all matters concerning the building had been placed in the hands of higher authorities. But he did offer us seats, listened, and phoned the contractors to ask that our windows be boarded up again first thing in the morning to protect our remaining possessions.

In the *Spectator*'s article on the June 8 fire, Mrs. Flanagan reported that she "didn't see anyone." (A month earlier, Columbia had terminated the daytime guard service at the building, so that Mrs. Flanagan was in charge of security between 8 A.M. and 4 P.M.) And Daniel Rosenblatt said that the fire "certainly is strange," adding that it would "extend the time of completion of the renovations, but not substantially." "Completion" is an odd word for him to have chosen, since apart from construction of a temporary roof and removal of some dangerous debris, renovations had not yet visibly begun. All in all, this fire confirmed the tenants' conviction that it would have been foolhardy to agree to live in a half-empty damaged building for an indefinite period of time.

Nena O'Neill, in whose living room the June 8 fire was set, had by that time "detached" herself. "At some point you've got to say, those are your losses. For a long time I tried to reclaim things, washed the covers of books, cleaned smoke-licked clothes and sheets, but after a while I said, This is ridiculous, what am I doing? I began to see the fire as really an omen. All I had been doing since George died was sorting through the material things of our lives. The omen was, It's time to move on, stop living in the past. Maybe I wasn't quite ready to let go then. I wanted to do it at my own pace, but you can't always do things at your own pace. Fate stepped in and rushed it along, so say good-bye to it.

"It sure was a bang-up way to close a chapter in my life, but I'm trying to turn a negative thing into a positive one. Clearing the way for new things to happen. They are only material possessions, but you still possess it all in your mind, all the past. Although things do evoke their memories. If you can touch them, you can get your memories back."

As soon as the negotiations collapsed, Columbia rescinded its offer of temporary housing. Harold Lurier, weeks earlier, had become "so disgusted" that he asked his brother Norman, in Buffalo, to write to the Housing Office about getting their mother an apartment. "They came to an agreement, I thought I'd go and sign for an apartment at the same low rent, and then it all hit the fan on a Monday morning. Moriarty said, 'It's all off, it's going back to court, my hands are tied.' " Rebecca Rikleen, still living in the West Sixty-eighth Street apartment with Ethan, had an appointment to look at apartments in early June, but she never got to see any.

Inge Irving had an appointment for June 11. When the Housing Preservation suit resumed in court on June 10, she remembers, "Byron Golden came over and said to me, 'Everything is off. You've taken us to court—all arrangements are off.' I had recently returned from Dallas, where I had to learn the computer system for my business. I hadn't really learned it—I was too distracted. It was also my heavy season, and then there was Debby's marriage on June 19. The worst of it was having friends and relatives come in for the wedding and not being able to put them up. We had looked forward to this."

Despite Inge's worries, Debby's wedding reception was a great success, held on a perfect bright afternoon, in a large, airy downtown loft and spilling out onto a rooftop terrace. Harry and I sat at a corner table with Nena and Jerry and Selma, drinking champagne and talking, inevitably, about the fire—we admitted we were obsessed. Nena remarked that wherever she went, she was happy to meet anyone who had been in a fire—"at last someone understands what I'm going through." We were all bedecked in summer finery—new clothes, of necessity—and talking energetically, even laughing at our predicament. I remember thinking that any of the ordinary guests looking on would never suspect . . . as if we harbored beneath our nice clothes a dirty stigma. Later, we walked out on the terrace and looked over the city and wondered where in it we might possibly live.

Our family was caught in that same bureaucratic warp. Since our hospitable friend needed her apartment back, we had arranged on June 4 to stay at a hotel for a month at Columbia's expense, and had confirmed this arrangement with James Kyrimes of the Housing Office. On June 12, unaware of the university's turnabout, the four of us and several carloads of stuff moved into the Hotel Esplanade, where Jerry and Selma once more became our neighbors. But when the first bill fell due, the hotel manager informed us that Columbia was refusing to pay it. Harry wrote to John Moriarty on June 30, asking that the commitment be honored, especially as our deposit had already been reimbursed by Columbia on June 20.

The following day, Moriarty left a telephone message at

Harry's office: "answer to your inquiry is NO."

Harry took the matter to Small Claims Court, where Byron Golden argued that the university had withdrawn its offer of hotel quarters the day the case resumed in Housing Court. On August 18 we were awarded $950 by the arbitrator (two weeks' charges less the $100 deposit). Believing the merits were thus settled, Harry then wrote to Columbia requesting reimbursement for the remaining two weeks in the hotel; since Small Claims Court has an upper limit of $1,500, we could not have sued for the entire amount at once. Byron Golden gave the same reply he had given in court, in a letter also warning that it would be illegal for us to sue twice over the same issue. Harry filed another suit in Small Claims Court (which was never heard because we were both sick when the case came up).

A few weeks after the second fire, the tenants set up a table on Riverside Drive to leaflet passersby. "Dear Neighbors," the handouts read, "How do you feel about living on the same block with an empty fire-damaged building that looks terrible and smells worse? As tenants and members of the community you deserve to live in a decent place. . . . In its present condition, the building is a hazard to the rest of the block and an invitation to another fire which could spread to other buildings."

Neighbors were asked to sign a form letter expressing their discontent and once more urging Columbia to restore 547 immediately. One hundred fifty of these letters were sent to President Michael Sovern in late June. A neighbor from 530 next door sent a personal letter: "Images of the south Bronx come to my mind, where one fire becomes a forerunner to other fires and unspeakable devastation ravages a community. . . . It seems to me that restoring the building would bring some stability to the tenants who were the victims of this terrible fire—and some stability to the community again." After a few weeks she received a reply from Claude Morton, vice-president for investments, saying that the university was equally desirous of having the building repaired promptly. "Unfortunately," Morton wrote, "pending litigation with several of the former tenants . . . has precluded . . . the modifications and repairs that it [Columbia] wishes to make."

Jerry Silverstein continued to spend most of his time apartment-hunting. "The thought of buying an apartment—because there's nothing around at a reasonable rent . . . Well, we were both from poverty-stricken families with a bargain-basement mentality, and to buy an apartment takes a tremendous removal from who and what you are. Almost all our married life was lived on that block, most of it in 547. The kind of camaraderie there was in the building . . . Why, with George and Nena we would be in there till five in the morning sometimes, talking away. And with the Uehlings—for several years we spent more time with them than with anyone else. It's like mourning—the end of the marvelous friendships, the end of your little nest. I remember, thirty-two years ago, I walked from super to super on Riverside Drive, and I gave the super in 530 ten dollars to hold the apartment. Now, every time I pass by 547, it's a *shteck in herzen.*" A stick in the heart.

9 Back in Court: Money and Words

The first item of business when the Housing Court case resumed on June 10 was amending the original petition to include repairs of damages caused by the June 8 fire. The trial continued with ten days of recitations by expert witnesses on the state of walls, wiring, beams, pipes, boiler, roof, and so on. It is unlikely that structural experts, even when testifying for opposing sides, can disagree dramatically on the condition of a wall or a boiler. But there were three issues raised by Columbia that peppered the dull proceedings: first, the ongoing claim that the court had no jurisdiction to order restoration of a building damaged by fire—to which Irwin Wiederkehr replied, "If this court does not have jurisdiction to hear this case then no court does"; second, that while the university had ample means available to restore the building, an order to do so would be "confiscatory," that is, an unjust financial burden, since 547 had been unprofitable in recent years; and last, that the Buildings Department order to repair raised a crucial semantic issue. *Repairing* the building, Byron Golden argued, possibly according to new plans, with a new layout, and for different occupants, was quite different from and more acceptable than *restoring* it to its original form and for its legal tenants. ("If that can happen," Kenny Schaeffer said, "I feel that there is no protection for the tenants of New York.")

Semantics arose first, as Wiederkehr opened the Housing Preservation Department's case by introducing into evidence and quoting from the March 3 Buildings Department violation: "Building damaged by fire . . . Remedy, make all necessary repairs as required," to which Golden responded:

> Your Honor, we object to the introduction of this document. This document is not just another one of a typical violation that commonly is presented to this court . . . that you didn't paint or another sort of insignificant violation. This violation is ambiguous, . . . very ambiguous. . . . This is broad, vague language. Necessary repairs as required. What does "as required" mean, your Honor? I respectfully submit that if we had the inspector here who gave it, we could inquire as to what was meant by that. . . . Does repair mean restore? . . . A repair, I respectfully submit, can be done by filing plans to alter this building and to repair the fire damage. If petitioners will concede that all they want Columbia to do is repair, fine, we will go ahead. We'd have no objection on that. They are asking for something more than repair. They are asking for an order of this court directing Columbia to restore.

The purported distinction demonstrated that the university was still seeking, as Wiederkehr put it, to "use fire damage to four apartments as a means of vacating an entire twenty-four-unit building of its legal tenants."

The judge accepted the document in evidence over Golden's objections, and the HPD case proceeded. Wiederkehr's first and only witness was James O'Brien, the HPD inspector who had accompanied Judge George on her trip to the building on April 4. O'Brien's purpose on the witness stand was simply to answer the question Wiederkehr later called "the bottom line: Are the repairs here feasible? Can they be made?" This took two days, partly because of Golden's unwillingness to accept the inspector as a qualified expert or the results of his visual inspection. Halfway through the first day of O'Brien's testimony, Golden moved to strike it entirely, "on the grounds that the inspection was conducted by the court and by the inspector with only one side being present." Wiederkehr rose to object. "Don't even get up," the judge said. Turning to Golden, she continued:

> This was already brought up. I admonished you before when you brought it up and I think it's really—I don't want to use the word childish, but it's very irritating that you keep going and harping on that. Now, I just really think it's just been said to death, and if you want to make any kind of motion at the end, make it, but I am not going to just ignore his testimony.

In the end, O'Brien reported what was apparent even to an unskilled eye: severe damage on the roof and the two top floors of the north wing, and largely cosmetic damage (requiring plaster and paint) on the south wing. He speculated that all the damage could be repaired within a few months.

Testimony by Columbia's major expert witnesses—Alvin Fischer and Richard Hill, both engineers—was ultimately not very different. At the start Fischer's testimony was somewhat dire: he seemed to believe that despite all the loose bricks having been removed and a temporary roof built, the north wing might still collapse and drag other portions of the building along. He also gave the impression that the task of rebuilding, including preliminary investigations, would be formidable. However, when Wiederkehr confronted Fischer with the report he had sent to Columbia, the situation sounded less grave. Fischer had written on March 8, "The apartments in the south wing sustained hardly any damage at all, except possibly from water and smoke. The roof over the south wing had some damage. Although the roof on the north side is almost completely destroyed, the masonry walls are still standing, however precariously. . . . Despite extensive damage, we found no evidence to indicate that the structure cannot be rehabilitated and rendered safe for habitation."*

Similarly, Richard Hill brought bad news about gas pipes and electrical lines, suggesting they might need to be replaced throughout the building. Then, when shown his inspection report, Hill stood by that March 30 assessment: many of the plumbing fixtures, pipes, and radiators were still acceptable; "damage to electrical installation in the south side apartments is minimal"; and the boiler in the basement appeared in good condition, except that its burner had been removed.

John Chandler testified that after the fire he had had the windows boarded up, the gas turned off, and the corridor doors chained, as well as arranged for temporary lighting in the hallways. After March 17, Chandler said, he was no longer responsible for the maintenance of 547. "It went to a new department . . . new construction." He had never seen or been told of the Buildings Department violation for the north wing, issued on March 3.

Columbia's remaining witnesses were hardly permitted to speak: the purpose of their testimony was to show the high cost of repairs, and in the earlier phase of the trial the judge had declared cost irrelevant since the university had the means to repair. John Weldon, an engineer and expert in "vertical transportation," was to have testified to the cost of repairing the elevator ($150,000, as Golden managed to slip in); Guenter Zagel, a Columbia building consultant, was to have specified the cost of particular repairs, apartment by apartment; and Allen Taylor, a Columbia real-estate investment officer, brought in what Golden called "a little sheet of paper" listing income and expenses for 547

*This was part of the preliminary engineers' evaluation of the building that Vice-President Morton had refused to make public at the Advisory Board meeting on March 22, which prompted the tenants' decision to file suit the next day.

over the preceding three years. When Wiederkehr objected to the sheet of paper on the grounds of its irrelevance, Golden explained:

> Here you have got a situation where a building has been losing money year after year. Can a court require expenditures in excess of one million dollars to be made just to put it back in the same condition so that the landlord can continue to lose money year after year? . . .
>
> MR. WIEDERKEHR: Your Honor, what would be relevant is not an income statement of this particular building, but an income statement of Columbia University. . . . If you have before you a landlord who . . . makes the argument that he is not required to provide heat and hot water or restore a building struck by fire because that building was losing money, what the court would have to do was to go behind that building, take into consideration the landlord's other assets, not only from his real estate enterprise, but his own personal assets, and that is how the court will determine the question.

In the end the judge sustained Wiederkehr's objection, "because I think this is opening up an aspect which goes to divide the court's attention from the main thrust of this case—whether or not to order repairs and restoration to this building."

When Golden saw his witnesses silenced one after another as they attempted to give figures, he moved, on June 21, to amend Columbia's formal answer to include cost as a defense. (A week earlier, after the petitioners had rested their case, the university had finally offered an answer to the original petition; the excuse for its untimely introduction was that Columbia had been hoping the case would be dismissed as not within the court's jurisdiction. Most of the seven points of the answer were stricken; in effect, cost *was* the only substantive defense.) To this suggestion of amending the answer, Kenny Schaeffer retorted:

> They not only wait three months to put in their answer, but now they, after the petitioner has rested and they call three witnesses, and they are trying to amend their answer. Assuming that they are conceding they can afford to do it and that it is physically possible, I don't think that cost is an issue as far as a statutory defense.

The motion to include cost as a defense was denied, "for the reasons . . . stated before." Golden immediately moved for a mistrial, also denied.

Despite the judge's firmness on this occasion, she had now and then allowed matters of cost to insinuate themselves, and so by the end of the trial it was common knowledge that repairs would amount to somewhere between $1 and $1.5 million, compared to $5 or $6 million to put up a new building on the site, and that Columbia had entered a claim for $2 million dollars in insurance —this fact slipped in by Wiederkehr. Moreover, all these figures were on the record, should Columbia need to appeal to a higher court.

The notion of improper jurisdiction had already been raised in April, to no avail. Golden repeated his motion to dismiss on those grounds on June 10. A written affirmation by Kenneth Block, another attorney for Columbia, attempted to support the position with precedents and documentation. None of the provisions of the Administrative Code, Block wrote—for example, to "keep premises in good repair" and to maintain safe conditions—"even hint that an owner is required to undertake the extensive restoration of a building substantially destroyed by fire." (In this "substantially destroyed" building, engineers for the university worked in offices in both the north and south wings; Mrs. Flanagan and her grandchildren hung out in the lobby; tenants walked in and out; telephone service continued; and Rebecca Rikleen kept stopping by to water her plants.)

Irwin Wiederkehr called Columbia's argument "inconceivable," citing the Civil Court Act that created the Housing Court:

> Specifically it states that the Housing Part has authority and jurisdiction to hear actions and proceedings involving the enforcement of State and local laws for the establishment and maintenance of housing. . . . This is exactly what we are doing here today.

In his written papers Wiederkehr pointed out that most of Columbia's precedents either involved commercial, not residential, properties, or did not come under the provisions of the Multiple Dwelling Law, or else occurred before the Housing Part of Civil Court was created and thus were decided under legislation now superseded. In addition, he noted that Columbia's most frequently cited precedent was decided before "the Housing Maintenance Code recreated a statutory duty to repair under a vacate order."

The judge denied Golden's June 10 motion to dismiss "because I feel this is the Court that was created to take care of just this item." Golden made the same motion two more times, first on June 15, adding that "The petitioner and respondent HPD have failed to prove a prima facie case," and again on the last day of trial, June 28, at which time Kenny Schaeffer, in a veritable seizure of simplicity, replied:

> Your Honor has been to the building with Inspector O'Brien. I think no doubt conditions exist which are not up to the code. And we have established that the tenants are tenants and that the landlord is the landlord, and I don't know what Mr. Golden is suggesting that we did not demonstrate.

The case was not dismissed. In his closing statement for HPD, Irwin Wiederkehr recalled that in an earlier case the court had held that a

> vacate order never contemplated the termination of the tenancies, nor did it contemplate termination of the landlord's duty to repair. . . . I think that the bottom line here has to be very simply the question, are the repairs here feasible? Can they be made? Every engineer who has testified here has stated that they could be made.

And for the tenants, Kenny Schaeffer argued:

> We are not talking about a building per se; we are talking about homes. There is a fire in this building on March 2, and the landlord for whatever reason has taken the position that it does not have to or does not want to restore these homes to their previous condition. As a result some fourteen rent-control families, some of them who have been there for forty years or more, some people in their eighties, are uprooted from their homes and are trying to get back in, and that's what this case is about. . . . The relief being sought is not punitive. . . . The landlord does not deny the building can be fixed, does not deny that it has the money to fix the building, and does not deny that it is fully insured. . . . The University apparently wants to take these homes away from these people, and that's why this case exists.

And the trial was over, except for a brief coda that led to complications later on. Kenny requested that the judge reinstate her order that the building not be demolished while her decision was pending, and that "no action be taken inconsistent with the granting of relief the tenants are seeking." Judge George responded:

> I think that my previous order still stands because I said it would be until the case is disposed of. . . . In the interim, I don't want any demolishing done unless it is strictly for safety. . . .
>
> MR. SCHAEFFER: Because of comments Mr. Golden made I would like clarification that there is no order right now that they not repair what they can repair.
>
> MR. GOLDEN: Your Honor, now we are going beyond—
>
> THE COURT: Now you are really going beyond. Just stop. I said I need time to go over all of these things.

This ambiguous order enabled Columbia, through the summer and fall, to continue to evade Criminal Court charges on failing to remedy violations.

Criminal Court handles a wide variety of civil violations, in Kenny's words, "down to the lowest level of illegal behavior, for example, jumping over turnstiles." By the end of June, the university had received six Criminal Court summonses for failure to comply with the Buildings Department repair orders for 547. (A summons is issued when a Buildings Department inspector visits the premises and finds violations of the Building Code.) In the seven months following the fire, Columbia appeared in Criminal Court to answer the violations on June 8, June 23, July 7, August 25, October 6, and October 24. Each time, Byron Golden succeeded in having the case postponed. The postponements were frustrating to the tenants, who organized small rotating groups to take off from work and appear in court. They were especially frustrating to Diana Angel, who attended every session of both Housing Court and Criminal Court—except when she was in Florida for her daughter's funeral—because she felt she lent credibility to the case.

Columbia's argument was that the conditions in the building were not violations subject to the Building Code and thus not within the jurisdiction of Criminal, or indeed any, Court. This was already familiar, but it was bolstered by a defense that astonished the tenants and their attorneys: that the university had been ordered by Judge George not to repair the building. Such an order, as the judge herself later commented, would have been bizarre: why should a Housing Court judge hinder a landlord from complying with a violation and satisfying the tenants? It would certainly dispose of the case in the simplest manner. But Columbia's strategy was to interpret in the broadest possible way the original court order of April 1, which, however ineptly expressed, was intended to protect the petitioners from finding a vanished or altered building, should they win the case:

> I want them to continue to make repairs only to the extent of safeguarding the area. I don't want them to further demolish or to go on or do anything else extensive. As far as putting up a temporary roof, I see no problem with that, and I will allow them to do that. They may not do anything else.

Not only in Criminal Court, but in the community as well, Columbia answered questions about the building with regrets that the tenants' willful rush to justice was preventing repairs.

In between the court sessions Harry wrote several times to Buildings Department Commissioner Robert Esnard, outlining the situation and urging the department to "take appropriate and prompt action in Criminal Court." On August 12 he wrote to Jeffrey Glen, special assistant to the New York City Corporation Counsel, calling Columbia's argument "preposterous," and asking that the city "vigorously prosecute" the case, "to help tenants who have been homeless almost *six* months." When the Criminal Court case next came up, on August 25, it was again postponed, on the same grounds.

In the meantime, after discussions in June, the city had agreed to bring an illegal-eviction suit against the university. The tenants believed, and the city evidently concurred, that the chaining of the doors and shutting off of utilities, as testified to by John Chandler, were grounds for such a charge, especially as no vacate order had been issued for the south side of the building.* "Had this been a private landlord," Kenny Schaeffer said, "he would long since have gone to jail for locking people out. Under the law

*This issue emerged as Chandler was being cross-examined on June 20: "Q. Did you check with the tenants with respect to chaining up the corridor doors? A. No. Q. Did you give a copy of the key to the tenants? A. No."

a corporation is to be regarded as a private person." In late July, Edward Faranda of the office of the Corporation Counsel promised that the suit would be filed within the next few weeks.

Apart from legal action, the tenants had long been seeking attention from the press; in late August they got it. A *Daily News* article called "Poison Amid the Ivy," by Bella English, described Columbia's practices as a landlord in a number of Morningside Heights incidents, the 547 fire among them:

> At 600 W. 113th Street, an 84-year-old woman lives in squalor in a single-room-occupancy hotel. For years, she said, she has waited for her landlord to fix up a larger room on another floor where she lived for 30 years before it was damaged by fire.
>
> Just around the corner, you can get a double-scoop ice cream cone for $2.20 at a Haagen-Dazs store—one of several chic new businesses that have popped up in the neighborhood in the last few years.
>
> Despite their obvious differences, the fancy ice cream store and the SRO have one thing in common: Their landlord is Columbia University.

Towards the end of the article, a Columbia vice-president is quoted as saying, "gentrification is inevitable," while a faculty-written report envisions that "by discreet use of property and facilities, Columbia and the neighboring institutions can make of the area a cultural center with some of the attraction of Greenwich Village, the animation of the Latin Quarter, the ethnic excitement of Chinatown." How this color and variety is to be sustained in a community eventually stripped of almost all but students and professors—who have not since perhaps the twelfth century in Paris provided the animation of the Latin Quarter—is not explained.

The tenants spent the summer of 1983 in a state of waiting—for action in the Criminal Court case and the eviction suit, but most of all for Judge George's decision. To Inge Irving, the months of uncertainty were "a ridiculous dilemma. I didn't pack up because I thought I'd get back in, I couldn't settle where I was, and I couldn't move because there was nowhere to go. I felt like a yo-yo, like I was being battered around constantly. In a city of transients and with a high-pressure job, you need one base, your own little kingdom that's yours. Oh, the building next door is a nice building too, but ours had a quality. . . . And besides that, it's a beautiful building, built by artisans, the best that came to this country. There was a kind of joy and thought to the architecture. The curlicues on the facade, the marble stairs. Nobody does that anymore. And they wanted to destroy it. It shows a disregard of life, a disregard of history. Think of all the life that building has housed. . . . Even now, the way it is, whenever I go into that lobby, I still see Ben there."

When their insurance money ran out in July, the Silversteins moved into Jerry's brother's apartment in the Bronx, the fourth of five temporary places. During the summer months, Selma would wake up in the middle of the night and remember some object she would never see again, and then she would see everything in the apartment in its place. Total recall, she called those nighttime visions, like a film she couldn't turn off. One night Jerry, too, sat bolt upright in bed. "I suddenly realized I would never see my father's shoes again. There's a story attached to those shoes. My father died while I was in the army, stationed in a chateau in France—this was in 1944, just after the fall of Paris —and I was nineteen years old. I was summoned to the office of the Catholic chaplain in the library of the chateau and wondered what dread deed I had done. The chaplain took me over to the French doors overlooking a field of snow and told me. He asked if there was anything I would like and I said I would like to walk in the snow for a while.

"I didn't see my family until January of 1946, a year and a half later. This was wartime, there were no leaves or furloughs. When I got home I asked, 'Did Papa leave anything?' They showed me a pair of shoes my father used to wear to the synagogue on holidays. I took them, and I took them with me when I got married. I would wear them to every family occasion and celebration—they fit perfectly—and I would say to people, 'Papa is with us tonight.' "

Judge George's decision came on August 26, two months after the trial ended. The strangest thing about it, in this age when millions of families own computers, was its seven handwritten pages—she had no staff person to type it for her.

> A vacate order has one purpose and that is to safeguard the life and safety and health of the occupants of a building. It does not alter the status of the occupants of the building. . . . This court finds no impediment to its granting petitioners' motion.

Victory for the tenants. The official court order, a month later, listed in voluminous detail all the repairs the university must make, and literally ordered Columbia to restore the individual tenants to their respective apartments, within four months for the south side and six months for the north—a more stringent schedule than the tenants had proposed during the unsuccessful negotiations four months earlier.

Was this case distinctive? I asked the tenants' co-counsel, Len Lerner. "Sure. You don't often have a case with a major burn-out and Housing Court requires the landlord to rebuild it." Could it be used as a precedent? "Yes, it could." And did he think there was any validity to Columbia's argument that this court had no power to order such rebuilding? "No. The purpose of the Housing Part is to safeguard the housing stock. From my point of view that was what it did. She enforced the law."

For the attorneys the case was not quite over. Kenny Schaeffer had seen the Criminal Court case postponed as a result of Byron Golden's claim that Columbia had been ordered not to repair the building. Fearing the university would use the same excuse when the case came up again on August 25, Kenny had gone to Judge George that morning and asked her to sign an affirmation stating: "There is no order from this Court restraining the landlord from repairing the building, 547 Riverside Drive, New York, New York, although there was an order that the building must not be further demolished, pending the disposition of HP 10115-83."

On August 26, on the basis of that affirmation, Byron Golden presented a motion for the judge's disqualification and recusal. "Judge George has permitted herself to be drawn into other litigation affecting the parties herein, has taken sides in that litigation, and has so manifested her prejudice against respondents that they cannot possibly receive a fair and impartial determination herein." Golden also asked that the judge's decision be deferred until the consideration of this motion; her decision, however, had already been issued that same day.

The university's timing and strategy—making a motion which would not be decided until September 13 (after Golden returned from vacation) rather than using swifter legal means available—were interpreted by Kenny Schaeffer in his written opposition "as a frivolous attempt to delay this proceeding further and to insult and embarrass the Court. . . . Judge George signed the affirmation not out of any desire to 'take sides' in the criminal proceeding, as Mr. Golden alleges, but to *prevent* her words from being taken out of context and fabricated into a nonexistent order used for partisan purposes by the landlord to obstruct another proceeding."

On September 13, Irwin Wiederkehr, Kenny Schaeffer, Byron Golden, and Judge George met in court to consider Golden's motion for recusal. "Your Honor," Golden began, "what's on my mind is what I consider to be a great breach of ethics by Mr. Schaeffer and a great breach of judicial ethics by this Court." Golden spoke at length justifying his interpretation of the judge's order, and referred to her signing the affirmation as a "star chamber" proceeding.

> The fact that Mr. Schaeffer made an ex parte* application came as no surprise; this is how he practices law. I was, however, shocked that this Court permitted itself to be drawn into that kind of unethical conduct, and in effect to perpetrate a violation of not only the canons of ethics but the constitutional rights of my client to a fair hearing.

Kenny, after pointing out the ludicrousness of an order not to repair—his clients would hardly request it, nor had the landlord—explained his behavior on August 25:

> I believe that Mr. Golden knew that there was no such order and was trying to take some words out of context in order to obstruct the proceedings of Criminal Court. And I felt obliged, both in the interest of my clients as well as the interest of justice, to prevent this obstruction from going forward. I don't think I did anything improper, and much more certain am I that this Court did not do anything improper. If Mr. Golden has any complaints about my behavior, there are forums where he could raise that and I'd be perfectly willing to defend what I did. But it has absolutely nothing to do with the decision that this Court has rendered on the case in chief in ordering that the homes of my clients be restored. . . . And I would add one more thing. If Mr. Golden is giving lectures on ethics, I would point out that it's he, ex parte, who sent a letter to the Court trying to introduce additional evidence after the record was closed.

(The reference is to a letter Golden sent the judge on July 15, asking her to "take judicial notice" of a violation forbidding anyone to live in 547 until a new certificate of occupancy was

*One-sided.

obtained, the building having stood vacant for more than sixty days. It was a letter Wiederkehr had also considered "highly improper." "For Columbia University," he wrote to the judge on August 5, "to imply and to argue that the placing of a violation by HPD on the premises . . . should in any way change the outcome of this trial or should in fact be considered by this Court is to plumb the depths of cynicism and hypocrisy when it is Columbia University's *own actions* which have caused the placing of this violation." In any event, the technicality obviously did not affect the decision.)

Irwin Wiederkehr confessed his mind "boggled" by Golden's use of the court order:

> Surprisingly enough to me, he [Golden] got a lot of mileage out of that. He got several adjournments. . . . I will concede, after looking at part of this transcript, that it may have been unclear, if one wanted it to be unclear. If one wanted to take a little crack in the language of the Court and ram a truck through, you could do it. And that's what Columbia University did. . . . What Mr. Golden would have to show here is that somehow your signing that Affirmation created a reasonable inference of lack of impartiality on the part of the trial judge. I don't see how this could possibly be construed in this manner. . . . Secondly, your Honor, and it pains me to say this, but I think Mr. Golden is just looking—was looking throughout the course of the trial—to manufacture evidence, another string to his bow on appeal. . . . I think your Honor bent over backwards to give Mr. Golden the benefit of the doubt in even listening to his oral motions for recusal. At some point I was waiting for the Court to hold him in summary contempt, if the truth be known. And for him to come in and say that there was a violation of judicial ethics, and to call this a star chamber proceeding, is just—it's terrible, your Honor. I think that anyone with any sense of fair play would never say that.

"Reasonable men," Golden responded, presumably alluding to the judges in the appeals court, "will have to read this transcript and they will decide. That's the American system of justice." He added that by the end of the trial he was convinced that "the case was going to be decided against me—your Honor's actions had made that clear. I didn't feel I had a crack at it, your Honor." At that point the judge ended the case with a rather unusual extemporaneous address:

> This was a long decision for me to make. . . . Until I finished writing it, I didn't know how the case was going to go. So if you knew how it was going to go, then you really should be at the racetrack, or some other place, because you have more talent than anybody. . . . When I came in here on August 26, it [the decision] was already in its final form. . . . I don't know when the court officer mailed it. I Xeroxed it and that's it. . . .
>
> Now, let's get to the issue here. As far as my recusing myself, I would only recuse myself if, as I stated here before when I was asked to recuse myself for different reasons in this case, if there was a reason under the statute, under the Judiciary Law, the Ethics Law. Not being related to anybody here in the fourth degree, or having any relationship, financial or otherwise, or any interest, or any sentimental attachment or any kind of involvement with any of these people, there'd be no reason for me to recuse myself. . . .
>
> And as far as this other business with Mr. Schaeffer, when Mr. Schaeffer brought this to me, I guess he could be criticized, because he came in here in a courtroom full of people as is the case, and he told me that this matter was on and that my words are being used, that I had issued an order not to correct. And I told him that I hadn't issued an order not to correct because there'd be no reason for me to tell somebody not to correct something which would result in the settlement of the case. . . . It's incredible that anyone would expect me to stand on that kind of a principle. On the other hand, and if you read all the minutes, you'll see that it is a little confusing, but in my mind, and I think if you read the minutes with an open mind, it'll always be that I said no more demolition or destruction, with the exception of fixing up any bricks that were falling or with putting up a temporary roof. . . . But that would not stop somebody from wanting to correct or repair, and I would never say, no, you can't till I decide

the case, because there'd be no issue then if they wanted to correct. Because, I mean, to me it boggles the mind and it's incredible that anybody would use my statement, and I just don't think that anybody should use my statement; if anything, you should have come here first, Mr. Golden, and gotten me to write something before you went and told the [Criminal Court] Judge what I said. I don't want my words bandied about, and if they're going to be bandied about, I'm the only one to bandy them. And I told Mr. Schaeffer that I wanted him to insert there that it was an ex parte application and I wanted him to insert the words that I put. Now, maybe Mr. Schaeffer was wrong. Maybe I was wrong, and maybe you were wrong too. But what happened in Criminal Court has nothing to do with that case that ended and upon which record and notes and exhibits and conduct during trial I based my decision. I didn't base my decision on Mr. Schaeffer's coming in here on August 25th. I mean, that to me is ridiculous. . . . I have to deny your motion to recuse myself and that's it.

On September 8, the *Spectator* reported that the university intended to appeal the case, and another period of limbo began. No repairs were started in the building, as far as anyone could see. While we waited, those tenants who had suffered the most damage to their possessions filed a $16.5 million negligence suit against Columbia. "Negligence" was based on the fact that tenants had called and written to the university's Housing Office many times over the years about the hazardous conditions in apartment 6C, where, according to the fire marshal's report, the fire began. Attorney David Lee predicted it might take eighteen months or more for the case to come to trial.

And Harry wrote again to the office of the New York City Corporation Counsel, on September 27:

As far as I know, although I would be delighted to be corrected, the papers [on the illegal-eviction action] have not yet been sent for service. I am sure that you realize the seriousness of the circumstances

> connected with the case. Almost *seven months* after the first fire and the University's illegal eviction of tenants from the south wing, several tenants do not yet have adequate temporary quarters. . . . We trust that the case, which the city agreed to file well over three months ago, will receive immediate attention.

And again in the same vein three weeks later.

A good turnout of tenants appeared in Criminal Court on October 6, when Columbia's violations case once more came up. To their chagrin it was once more postponed, after the university argued that the problem did not fall within the jurisdiction of Criminal Court. The judge asked attorneys on the staff of the Corporation Counsel to submit, within a week, a short written refutation of Columbia's argument.

The tenants were not at all sure, by now, whether they had anything to celebrate; still, they went ahead with plans for a victory party on Saturday afternoon, October 8, to be held in Riverside Park at Grant's Tomb, up the street and across the Drive from 547. It was a place where everyone's children had ridden bikes, tossed balls, and slid down the monument's slopes on snowy days, though few had ventured into its dull depths. For the past ten years or so a ring of new benches had surrounded Grant's Tomb, amoeba-like concrete benches with a sense of humor, studded with multicolored mosaics—artifacts of pop culture and the local scene, from Batman to a New York City taxicab. The tiles were put in place by various community groups; our younger daughter, Miranda, had worked on them when she attended the nursery school of the epic walking pool. Oddly enough, the gaily decorated, curvaceous benches had themselves, not long before, been a matter of contention. Descendants of General Grant felt they demeaned his dignity, and perhaps they did, but somehow—with or without litigation—they managed to remain. They were bizarre, beautiful and ugly, classy and vulgar, rather like a clump of Gaudí structures, and they certainly didn't fit in with the general stolidity, but they did grow on us all. Doubtful at first, we had come to love them, and now, on this gloriously amber fall day, they made fine tables for platters of food. Diana Angel brought trays of assorted sandwiches, Jerry Silverstein brought roast chickens, Christian Regelin brought potato salad Joan had made. Lots of people brought wine. Earl Brown, from Borough President Andrew Stein's office, came; he had been interested in the case from the start. Neighbors passing by were pulled in to join the party. Kenny Schaeffer came with his wife, who was pregnant, and their young daughter. We presented Kenny and Susan with a gift certificate for the coming baby, but he demurred since he was in the employ of an elected official. We all ate a lot and refilled our glasses and toasted to getting our building back; we tried to believe we had won a victory. At least the waiting for the decision was over. Now there was just the other waiting.

It might take many months to learn the results of Columbia's appeal, which was officially filed on October 13. Meanwhile, our landlord, like any other, was still required to comply with the court order to repair. The logical step for the university would be to seek a stay of the order, which would permit a delay on rebuilding until the appeal was decided. This was done on October 26, in written papers arguing again that the court had no jurisdiction to order restoration of a building damaged by fire. Irwin Wiederkehr wrote in opposition, again supporting the court's jurisdiction and going through Columbia's precedents one by one to distinguish them from the case in hand. One comparison is especially pungent. "This case can be distinguished from *Harmor Operation Co.* v. *Vent-O-Matic* in that the alternatives here are not between repair or demolition of the building. Columbia has not indicated that it intends to remove its property from the housing market, only that it wishes to tenant it with different individuals." Wiederkehr enunciated what everyone was reluctantly beginning to suspect—that if a stay was granted, the tenants' "victory in the court [would] be a hollow and Pyrrhic one." Given the possibilities of vandalism and arson, as well as the caprices of weather, "the longer the building stands unrepaired the greater the danger that the tenants . . . may never have homes to return to. . . . It is well settled law," he added, that if a stay is so prejudicial as to turn the winner into the loser, it should not be granted.

"All three branches of the state government," Kenny wrote in his opposition, "the legislature through the enactment of Multiple Dwelling Law Sec. 78, the executive through the New York City Building Department orders to repair, and the judiciary through the judgment below, have independently created an obligation on the part of the landlord herein to repair this building. Appellant cannot argue to this Court that compliance with the law is prejudicial, especially when that compliance is required three different ways."

But evidently appellant could, and did.

10 A Season of Discontent

The period of waiting during the fall months was especially harrowing to Inge Irving, since the friend whose rent-controlled apartment in 548 Riverside Drive she was using had recently received an eviction notice from Columbia. Inge called this a "double devastation." Under New York State regulations, however, tenants in rent-controlled housing cannot be evicted. Harry brought the matter up at a November meeting of the Advisory Board in Riverside Church. From the minutes:

> This, Harry said, is especially inhumane, adding insult to injury. Wasn't it bad enough that Inge Irving had to suffer the hardship of being burned out of her apartment and having to relocate somewhere else? We can only speculate as to what might be behind such a hideous action on the part of the University.
>
> Greg Fusco [vice-president for government relations] stated that it was his information that the case involved a lack of affiliation on the part of the tenant of record. . . . Fusco expressed some doubts on an easy resolution of the matter.

But inquiry confirmed that the tenant concerned was in fact protected by rent control and no affiliation clause was involved. The eviction proceedings were dropped a week later. At the next board meeting, Vice-President Claude Morton called the attempted eviction "the result of an unfortunate misunderstanding. Had the tenant in question informed the University directly of their standing as a tenant, the situation could have been avoided."

In the first week of November 1983, Columbia was granted a stay on Judge George's order to rebuild 547 Riverside Drive. The university's appeal would probably not be heard until around March of 1984, a year after the fire; thus the building would remain empty and deteriorate for five more months, while the tenants' future remained uncertain. Kenny Schaeffer seemed as downcast as his clients at the news. Spirits reached a new low as everyone grasped that the Housing Court decision might be a victory only on paper. As one tenant noted, "The impact of the beginning, when people feel sorry for you, passes. Even the neighbors on the street. I thought people should be more agitated, I told them it could happen to them. But you can't expect them to understand. I've wondered, though, are the trustees aware of how these people at Columbia are behaving?"

Coula Lurier flew to Nassau.

Diana Angel planned a trip to Washington in December to work on a wedding dress for her grandniece and Mrs. Lurier's granddaughter, who wanted to wear the same dress Diana had made years ago for her mother. Diana grumbled cheerfully that it would be no easy task to alter the dress since the bride was four inches shorter than her mother. "Still, this means something. On the one hand we have death, and then we have this. We have to figure out a way to start our lives again."

After much looking around, Rebecca Rikleen sublet an apartment for herself and Ethan in Washington Heights, in a neighborhood she liked. "All the time I wasn't working at The Red Balloon I was either looking for someplace to live or going to tenant meetings. I feel as if I've had no free time since March

2. It became very depressing, an insidious kind of depression that hangs there and doesn't go away because of the feeling of being out of control over what's happening. The way we let ourselves be led on stripped us of our self-respect and made us feel impotent. Or maybe I should say made me, anyway.

"I was never attached to material things, but I began to feel I needed some kind of permanence, some kind of nest that's mine. I also did not feel wedded to this building. I was willing to move elsewhere, but I couldn't find suitable housing I could afford. Vacancies are being held all over the city by landlords who want to go co-op. Also there are old and single people staying on in very large apartments who don't dare move because they know they won't find another place. It's all very cruel and unfortunate.

"Ethan doesn't talk about it. At the beginning, after Chris and Daniel left and I told him I didn't want to stay alone in the school at night, he gave up his sleepovers with his friends and stayed there with me without complaining. But since we moved to the apartment in Washington Heights he has avoided coming home; he stays out with his friends. I once said to him, 'You never come home before I do. You don't like your home.' He said, 'I don't feel it's my home. We don't have a home.' "

At a Columbia street fair that fall, Kenny Schaeffer ran into Larry Dais. Afterwards, Kenny told Harry they had discussed the appeal. Both had agreed it was "a pity" that the tenants still had no permanent homes and that the two sides couldn't settle between themselves. "Then I met Moriarty at Columbia," Harry recalls. "This was purely accidental—I was seeing an old friend about something entirely different and Moriarty happened to drop by. He was courteous but reserved, which he is generally. We had won; he didn't attempt to establish any superiority. But of course he didn't congratulate me either. He said he wasn't involved in it any longer, but we did get to talking kind of frankly." In the end, there was the possibility of negotiating again.

As Harry saw it, Columbia had more reason to be conciliatory now than in April, since the tenants had won a "pretty resounding decision." Besides the considerable legal expenses involved, the appeal was risky. If the university won, it would have the entire building for its own use. But if it lost, it would have only a dozen apartments scattered through both wings and much more difficult to renovate individually—and possibly for students—than the entire north wing the tenants had been willing to concede.

As far as the tenants were concerned, despite the decision, nothing was happening to the building and might not for some time. Even if Columbia lost on appeal, rebuilding would probably not start till the following spring, that is, in 1984. There was the possibility, too, that the university might win a new trial, or appeal to a still higher court. Either way, Harry felt, "time was not on our side. Negotiating is much quicker. I realize there's the attitude of pride, of not giving in in any way, leaving it strictly to the courts—a few of the tenants felt this way. But I saw a number of people still suffering, not happy where they were, living in hardship. I thought that had more weight than a principle or pride.

"I told Moriarty there was no sense in negotiating if they wouldn't agree on a date to fix the whole building. He was a little different this time; there was some greater deference or respect, yes. He didn't say things like, What's your interest in the north wing?—some of his old lines. He said he'd talk to Vice-President Anthony Knerr, who's the second in command on the business side, and see if they were willing to negotiate. Later I told Kenny what had happened. We figured, two accidental meetings like that—it was certainly worth a try."

In their discussions, the tenants agreed, without great enthusiasm, to "see what they had to say." Those who might have preferred to stand on principle didn't want to prevent others from getting their apartments back. And no one relished the alternative, which was to wait for the outcome of the appeal. As before, any agreement reached would be signed under the aegis of the court and have the force of a court order. It was felt that in this round of negotiations the group would be best represented by Len Lerner, who had been acting in an advisory capacity all along, rather than by Kenny Schaeffer, whose relation to Columbia is usually adversarial.

Len Lerner works in a neat, unpretentious office near Lincoln Center on Manhattan's Upper West Side. In his waiting room, along with several prints reminiscent of Daumier, hangs a large movie poster for a film called *Justice Takes a Holiday,* and in his office, among the stacks of lawbooks and journals, is a copy of Bruno Bettelheim's *The Uses of Enchantment.* Len is a short, well-dressed man in his fifties, with thick glasses, longish graying hair, and a confident and chivalrous, if loud, manner.

During the case, many of the tenants had found Len "difficult," meaning he was authoritative and impatient, he lost his temper, he raised his voice—all of which he doesn't deny. "Sometimes tenants are driven by emotional desperation to let off steam at me and yell, and on occasion, yes, I yell back. I'm used to it, not that I like it. But you're sitting on a keg of dynamite when you're dealing with people's homes. In this case, at times it was very uncomfortable, I'll put it that way, because of the pressure on my clients that they vented on me. One night, after a meeting that ended at eleven-thirty, when I was very excited, Harry and Inge took me out for a cup of coffee to calm me down. I appreciated that very much.

"But I know how it feels. My own family's been evicted twice. Once, when I was a kid, my father was out of work during the

Depression and we were almost put out on the street. Then my father was evicted from his store in November of 1971. He'd had that store since 1939. The landlord wanted four times the rent. I tried but there was nothing I could do about it. There are no controls on renting commercial property in New York, so this kind of thing is happening all over the city—the small shops are pushed out and the fancy boutiques move in."

Despite its inevitable pressures, defending tenants has become a major part of Len's practice, what he's most known for. "I never was personally involved in politics, but during the Vietnam war I did a lot of reading and thinking. I spoke against it at the beginning, at a time when you could get a lot of abuse, and I did. I noticed that decent people who felt the same way had joined the local Democratic club and I took the jump and joined—it was during the Eugene McCarthy campaign. Then they asked, was there any lawyer in the club, could I come to the clubhouse on Monday and Thursday nights to advise people on housing problems? Now, I didn't know anything about housing, but I did it as a volunteer and over the years, with all the studying, I became knowledgeable. I got involved with housing groups, I was one of the original founders of the West Side Tenants Union. Finally I incorporated it all into my work and my life. Often landlords, seeing me in court, have asked me to represent them, and I say, No, I represent tenants. I don't want to make a hundred thousand dollars. My clients can't pay that. People ask me, Why don't you charge more and make more? and I say, If you have to ask that, you don't understand what I'm after. My soul's got to eat too."

Reopening the negotiations on 547 Riverside Drive provided food for the body as well. Byron Golden invited Len to lunch on November 4, "at the Harvard Club, if that's of any importance, but it does show he wanted to make a good impression. We were feeling each other out. Golden and I have had cases before—

we've always treated each other with respect and courtesy."

As before, the negotiations between the attorneys entailed a series of meetings, phone calls, and successive draft agreements passed back and forth for tinkering. Although the tenants were not participating they were still vocal, even more distraught, and hoped to stretch the agreement to cover the ramifying complexities of their situations. "I would talk to the group up at Sullivan's office," Len recalls, "and each time someone would come up with something new to put in the papers. Finally I said, Please, give me the whole story; that's not how you negotiate. Because I would have to go back to Golden and say, Listen, there's one more thing I forgot. These are all nice people here; you can do this one more thing."

Before this round of negotiations began, the tenants had been planning a protest demonstration, in cooperation with the Morningside Tenants Federation, to be held in front of Columbia president Michael Sovern's East Side residence. One of the frustrations ever since the fire had been from Sovern's apparent indifference to community petitions as well as to the urgings of political leaders. Holding a demonstration where Sovern lived rather than on campus, the tenants thought, would be a more potent statement about their being homeless after nine months and a favorable court decision. Besides, the Columbia campus and its environs had been the setting for so many demonstrations that protesters were barely noticed. The Morningside Tenants Federation was eager to join in and link the 547 issue with other complaints about Columbia's housing policies.

As talks between the attorneys proceeded, though, we wondered if the protest would exacerbate relations and wreck an agreement at the critical moment. At one of the Thursday-night meetings it was decided that, all things considered, to date our predicament had not changed, nor had our feelings. December 10 was crisp and bright. The area we had reserved for the protest was blocked off by police barricades, and several policemen and women were on hand, whether to keep us orderly or to protect us was unclear. They were a friendly bunch, amused by our signs and our slogans ("President Sovern's house is neat, Columbia puts us on the street"; "We don't want a company town"; "Black and white, young and old, Columbia puts us out in the cold"); they counseled us, for future reference, that these days protesters bring coffee for the cops, something we had overlooked. About fifty people turned out, from babies in strollers to Diana Angel, who offered to appear in a wheelchair if that would make a greater impact. Her offer declined, she marched for two hours with the delight of one discovering her métier—"I'm eighty years old and this is my first protest!" She told Inge it was the happiest day of her life. Madison Avenue's Christmas shoppers, in furs and Chesterfields, stopped to gape at the motley, multicolored group, and perused the signs and accepted fliers in bafflement. An envoy was sent to the doorman, asking to see Sovern; the answer came back that he handled business at his office on campus.

The following day a *Daily News* article cited demonstrators' complaints of "a variety of tactics including illegal evictions, lockouts and harassment to get rid of them. . . . School officials say the evictions are necessary to help ease a projected housing crunch for students and university employees."

Like most protests, this one was exhilarating. And like many, it seemed neither to arouse the citizenry nor to hinder the formal machinery of compromise. At the January 5, 1984, meeting of the Advisory Board, Claude Morton reported that "Columbia has committed itself to restoring the building," and that tenants would be able to return to their apartments within six months. According to the minutes, Tom Kappner remarked that "it had appeared, several times in the past, that an agreement was imminent with only a few minor details remaining. He and others had had their hopes raised, only to discover later that the details had become major stumbling blocks."

But in mid-January, Columbia prepared a press release announcing a satisfactory agreement. "We are particularly pleased," Vice-President Anthony Knerr stated, "because the settlement meets our objective of improving the quality of life for all our tenants—both those affiliated with the university and those who are not." The release mentioned that although Columbia had opposed the Housing Preservation suit, "it continually and publicly favored the expeditious return of the tenants to a safe building." There was no mention that the tenants had won the suit.

The agreement provided that the university would repair the building—the south side by October 31 (nine months away, rather than the six Morton stated), and the north side by December 31, 1984. Tenants formerly living on the south wing would return to their apartments, while north-wing tenants would move across the hall to comparable apartments which before the fire had been either vacant or occupied by Columbia affiliates. All tenants would retain the privileges and protections of rent control and pay their former rents, except for small surcharges for any improvements made in order to fulfill the agreement; for example, if rewiring was necessary and resulted in more electrical lines and outlets, the tenants would pay an increase of perhaps three dollars a month. Until October 31, the university would continue to provide temporary housing as necessary, and would also pay for storing the tenants' possessions during the rebuilding. Among the minor points, our family was reimbursed for the hotel bill incurred seven months earlier.

Apart from the arrangements that concerned the tenants directly, the key provision, which Tom Kappner had warned against nine months earlier, and which we as tenants were powerless—

or too exhausted—to oppose, was: "Landlord shall have the right to subdivide the existing apartments in the north one-half of the premises into smaller, class 'A' units."

The tenants' responses to the document varied; mostly there was grudging satisfaction. "It should have been done a long time ago," Inge said. "I just want to see that it's fulfilled. Columbia University over this year has made me a more cautious person. I don't believe anything even if it's in black and white." Those who had felt most aggrieved all along continued indignant. Joan Regelin said, "The meetings left off in December and that was it. Three weeks later we get a letter in the mail from Harry saying we have reached an agreement. We were presented with the news after the fact; I tried to make my views known but they were discarded; furthermore, we were told if we don't sign we would be keeping the others from getting their apartments back. So we signed it. Yet there were several points I think could have been worked out. For example, our paying what are essentially their expenses: new wiring is to the benefit of the building and the landlord. Chances are, the insurance money will more than cover whatever they'll do. Then, our expenses were never paid—they were considered a different category simply because we didn't stay in a hotel, which I found very unjust. And why are we even paying legal expenses for an agreement which basically I find unsatisfactory? We could have said, You pay our court costs and attorneys' fees. Still, probably the only way we could have gotten anything would be with an agreement out of court. I was for it, only having been told after the fact was quite a blow. I signed that agreement under duress."

Len Lerner, reasonably enough, found the agreement fair and satisfactory, given the circumstances. Given, that is, that there was a fire in the first place, which some tenants, Len felt, refused to accept. In the end we all signed, with our varying degrees of satisfaction; no one wanted to keep his or her neighbors from going back home. We all knew, too, that no agreement would ever be really satisfactory. Nothing would, except somehow changing history so that it all had never happened.

On February 13, 1984, less than a month after the agreement was signed, the *Spectator* featured an article headed: "Fifty Students to Live in Redone 547." In it, Vice-President Anthony Knerr called the breaking up of the twelve north-wing apartments "an opportunity we needed to take advantage of."

I sat with Inge in a coffee shop and we passed the paper back and forth across the table, stunned. We shouldn't have been, of course; it was hardly news. Nonetheless, seeing it at last in front-page black and white, after all those months of struggle . . . "The whole character of the building will be gone," Inge said. "Them on one side, us on the other. It's a kind of segregation I don't like. They might at least have thought of young faculty members with families, who are in a bind."

When I next saw her weeks later, in fact a year after the fire, Inge summed it up: "I don't want to live in a dorm."

11 A Year Later

A year after the fire, Nena O'Neill has turned her office into a small studio she can live and work in. The study seems uncannily as I remember her study in 547—white walls, white desk, several white file cabinets, piles of papers neatly arranged. The living area is mostly white too, with furniture more sleek and modern than the old. Many of the Latin American decorations are gone, but there is a new honey-colored leather chair from Brazil. The shelves of books also look familiar, one shelf holding translations of *Open Marriage* in over a dozen languages. She points out a poster announcing a show of her older son's work. Michael is a photographer. The poster shows, slightly larger than life, gloriously lucid and meticulous, a scrub brush, a bar of wet soap, and a few drops of glistening water—the simple things taken out of context somehow infused with a special significance. She talks proudly about her other son, Brian, an anthropologist working in a village in Portugal—she visited him there the summer following the fire. Nena is wearing purple pants and a Mexican belt, and looks trim and young and happy, which she attributes to feeling generally better about her life, as well as to running in Central Park every morning at seven.

"I didn't feel as antagonistic towards Columbia as other people," she says. "I don't know if they should have been totally responsible for housing us, except that every institution has an obligation to the community, and they certainly could have extended themselves in some way during the crisis. Of course, you couldn't expect them to have our best interests at heart, but . . ."

A year after the fire, a few tenants are still living in cramped temporary quarters, with their belongings in storage. "At my age," says one, "I've lost two years of my life. I can't invite friends over. My Christmas this year was no Christmas. I didn't do anything, I completely let it pass, outside of going to church. Didn't even send cards. I just had no enthusiasm like other years. It messed up my life."

A year after the fire, it seems Inge still keeps a spirited indignation, despite the admonitions of the Reverend Coffin. "The narrow-minded and stupid way they behaved, for example, not repairing the roof right away. It was outrageous that no one represented Columbia University with any authority. The president didn't even honor the people in the community he was in. It was the worst public relations anyone could do. It was also one of the worst shocks of my life. And the irony is that by the time you're ready to get it back, you feel like saying, You can keep your goddamned apartment. . . ."

A year after the fire, Joan and Christian and their three children are still living in a temporary apartment on 115th Street, waiting for October 31 to move to the south side of 547. Joan says, "When I said before that the tenants' meetings were not worth a damn . . . I mean, in retrospect, how they affected me, my emotional energies. Of course we had no alternatives. It was the only way to accomplish anything, to organize and present a united front. Also, I was doing performances during that entire period. I was bringing my anxieties to everything else, rather than to the performances. Yes, there was a point where we were very close, for example at one of our Chinese dinners, when Selma said, Why don't we all buy a co-op together. And we still certainly have a rapport with one another, yet it seems to me we broke up into factions.

"I'm not angry at the individuals involved but at this corporation, which not only used the fire to victimize and manipulate us but put us in the position of dealing with them in this way, groveling, paying our attorney for their profit.

"As a family, this was probably the biggest trauma that happened to us. It was a strain on the kids, they each showed it in different ways, but they got through it okay. Their reactions stemmed from ours—they didn't get to see much of the fire itself. And Christian and I are very different personalities. We see things differently and approach them differently. I, from the moment it happened, felt myself very involved and felt responsible for being involved. I felt a great injustice had been done. He felt the same but was more able to take it in stride. I suffered tremendous stress and spent many sleepless nights worrying about what would happen to us. I even had nightmares about the piano being totally destroyed. All in all, it occupied our energies in a very destructive way, for a very long time."

A year after the fire, Harry says, "As these things go, I would say we worked together pretty well. We had all suffered this tragedy together—we had a common adversary. And the way Columbia acted helped to unify us—they were obstinate, immovable, completely uncompassionate. There were very different kinds of people and they took on different tasks—hiring a lawyer, doing publicity, telephoning, Xeroxing, and so on. There were some who didn't say much, and about half didn't do too much, but everyone understood the situation and where we were at different points. Nobody went off and got disgusted. And most of the time there was pretty good humor—certainly at our Chinese dinners. Of course, there was a kind of futility underlying it too, since all our efforts were just to get back what we had, not to be any better off. Everyone would be worse off, in fact. Still, we stuck together for over a year, we won in court, we got a reasonable settlement, and everyone got a place to live. Up to those few weeks at the end, with the bitterness over the agreement, I had a good feeling about it. Just those last few meetings . . . I still have a good feeling, though. I guess time will heal it all.

"As far as my personal life? Well, *you* know. It disrupted it. It took a year out of my life. A year. All the waiting, the uncertainty over where to live, all those temporary moves . . . I thought the hotel was the worst, by the way. I didn't like having to walk past the desk each time I went in and out, with someone watching. Things between us, seeing the kids suffer—it was probably the worst family trauma, and the most sustained. The one that will change our lives the most.

"I felt very attached to that building and that neighborhood after more than eighteen years and all that happened to us. It was not ideal. But it was unusual for New York: it was quiet, had a view, a lot of light. It belied the things they say about New York. All the little things too—rituals, seasonal stuff, people you knew by sight, the shopkeepers, the kids who were born there and grew up. The men playing dominoes and cards outside of the El Morro Social Club; the sign in the G & O butchers about getting your Thanksgiving turkey early, the same every November; the school bus at the corner in the mornings, year after year. Seeing the seasons change in Riverside Park. The snow there was very pretty to walk in. And the sunsets, let's not forget that.

"The suddenness—one day you don't have this awful thing in your life and the next day you do, and then you have it for a long time. And needlessly, lest we forget. That's something we try to avoid thinking about. That Evelyn . . . well, irresponsible is a pretty mild word!"

A year after the fire, Harold Lurier is busy translating four fourteenth-century Byzantine fairy tales from the Greek, "a strange Greek with Arabic influences. The stories have magic apples in them. Magic apples!" He waves his arms with a wild irony. "I'd much rather be thinking about fairy tales and magic apples than all of this!" Animated and outgoing, seemingly borne aloft on swift currents of words in a throaty voice that commands attention, Harold moves about as he speaks and everything becomes drama, performed with dialogue and gesture. Very likely he is the kind of professor who holds students enthralled. He relates that in December of 1983, when the settlement seemed near, he wrote to Daniel Rosenblatt of the Columbia Housing Office, who replied, "Come see me about housing." "Rosenblatt was wonderful and genial. He told his assistants, 'We want to take care of Mrs. Lurier.' Weeks went by. They sent me to terrible places, one on Amsterdam and 119th with a broken door, one on Claremont which was tiny. I wondered, Why can't I get something near the house? I asked the super in 528 Riverside Drive, just down the block, and found a vacancy. Then at the Housing Office they said, Oh yes, there's a vacancy there. They said the rent was $379. They gave me a runaround regarding the rent and complications with the senior citizens' subsidy. Then at one point they said they'd get it straightened out and asked me to take their word for it and sign. I said, Do you really expect me, at this point, to take your word for it? I waited another week. Finally I signed, after much haggling over the rent, the subsidy, and whose name appears on the lease. And then—they gave me the wrong keys!"

Mrs. Lurier was given the two-bedroom apartment in February 1984. Even though Harold has moved most of his mother's things in, she is still with her daughter in Washington because he hasn't had time to unpack all the cartons he packed after the fire. He says he has been working at it for a week, putting aside the magic apples, from seven in the morning till eleven at night: he must get everything unpacked before his mother arrives because she remains too weak from her illness to do any work. "I've been going crazy, moving all that stuff. She saves everything—cartons of papers, old bills, pictures.

"My mother was content, all those months, to keep moving; she likes to travel, but of course she became more morose, angrier. She never mentions the fire, but she does want to know about her apartment. She asks, 'What's it like?' and she reminds me, 'Don't give anything away.' By now, since nothing was done after that second fire last June, the ceilings have all fallen down on top of her stuff. It's a mess; the furniture is spoiled. You can't open the drawers of the cabinets because the wood is swollen. The jambs have opened up and the doors and windows have pulled away. The floors are bad. No, I had no insurance.

"About Columbia, I agreed with Joan that we mustn't let them off the hook, though I wouldn't have expressed myself in quite the same way. In my case, if they had offered me a decent apartment in the beginning, I would have taken it willingly. But they lied to me, cheated me, hung up on me, which was completely uncalled for. After that I would have fought it to the ends of the earth. But look, it's a corporation mentality, whether the business is Columbia University or the medieval church: its business is just to keep going.

"A friend told me last year, 'Harold, a year from now, mark my words, that building will be exactly the same.' And look at it!"

A year after the fire: The illegal-eviction suit which the city promised in June of 1983 to bring against Columbia, and about which Harry wrote in July, September, October, and December to the Corporation Counsel staff, somehow was never filed. Theoretically, Kenny Schaeffer explains, the case could still go forward. "It's like getting a parking ticket; you've moved your car from the offending spot, maybe even sold it by the time your case comes up, but you still have to pay the fine for the violation." In actuality, though, it is most unlikely that with new cases arising daily, the city's lawyers will ever press forward on this one.

In August of 1984, nearly a year after the tenants initiated their negligence suit against Columbia, the taking of depositions began, which means each side questions the other under oath. This procedure is still going on as I write, and promises to be lengthy, since the university's attorneys question each tenant closely on every item claimed to be lost or destroyed. Once the depositions are completed, the case will be placed on a trial calendar; tenants' attorney David Lee compares this to getting a number in a bakery. The traffic in this particular bakery being what it is, the waiting period for trial would ordinarily be fourteen to sixteen months. But because the case involves a tenant over seventy years old, the petitioners will be entitled to special preference and an immediate jury trial in New York State Supreme Court, "immediate" meaning in three or four months' time.

In September of 1984, a year and a half after the fire, Columbia's Office of Real Estate Management announced that it would establish at least one full-time social work position to deal with tenants "who sometimes create fire and health violations in university-owned residences." Vice-President Gregory Fusco pointed out that the university "has no legal responsibility to assist tenants with any social problems they might have," but added, "I'm glad to see us go that extra mile."

And towards the end of 1984, according to the office of the New York City Corporation Counsel, the Criminal Court case against Columbia for failure to comply with Buildings Department violations was resolved. The defendant paid a $17,000 fine.

The fall 1984 term found the university's housing problem notably improved. In a September 11 *Spectator* article headed "Despite Crunch, CU Houses Most Students Ever," President Sovern commented: "We are, in fact, housing significantly more graduate students than we were, I guess, against any base year. It has been a steady upward creep." Success was attributed to two causes: administrative efficiency and "the 52 new places that became available in 547 Riverside Drive this summer when the University completed renovations on the fire-damaged building."

The word "completed" once again was not entirely accurate. Renovations on the north side, transformed from twelve spacious apartments to twenty-four little ones, had indeed been finished and graduate students settled there in time for the opening of classes. But the south side, "our" side, looked in September 1984 virtually as it had the day after the fire eighteen months before. The negotiated agreement of the previous winter had provided that the south side would be completed by October 31 and the north side—for which Columbia had always claimed it needed more time—by December 31. But in the rebuilding process the priorities and lengths of time required somehow got reversed.

12 Being Erased

The last week in October, a few days before we were legally entitled to return to our renovated apartments, I visited the building. The outside concrete and brick work had been newly cleaned and the facade looked spiffy, although the ornamental cornice at the roof was gone, replaced by simple layers of brick. The front doors were new. Inside, the lobby was freshly painted, a peachy-rose color; an array of new steel mailboxes lined the wall—more mailboxes than ever before; and Mrs. Flanagan's young grandson, presiding at a desk, greeted me. The south side was still in the process of renovation: its halls had not yet been painted and workmen with equipment traipsed about. Mrs. Flanagan appeared and offered to show me around.

She took me to the north side first, which had new metal corridor doors and freshly painted walls. It was unrecognizable, a new construction on the old site. After walking down a long hall on the first floor we came to four doors, each a new and newly occupied apartment. There were one- and two-bedroom units, Mrs. Flanagan explained, for the students; all the kitchen and bathroom fixtures were new, and Columbia provided the basic furnishings. She said they were beautiful apartments. Then we went up in the elevator to see my sixth-floor apartment. It was the familiar old elevator, working despite the ominous trial testimony of the expert in vertical transportation, but Mrs. Flanagan said a new elevator would soon be installed.

Our apartment was completely empty. The walls had been scraped, plastered, and sprayed an ashy sort of white, the color of plaster of paris. No enamel had been brushed on those interminable wooden moldings; well, it did take a lot of time, I could vouch for that. The windows were new, with ugly black metal frames, and fireproof. The floors were newly scraped and polished; on the floor of the living room, where water had leaked in for almost two months from a hole in the ceiling, were black splotches, ineradicable. The bathroom fixtures had been cleaned, gone from black to their original white; the ones in the kitchen not yet, but the kitchen did have a new linoleum floor, one we would never in a million years have chosen, a cheap, hideous pale green, patterned in squares, with inverted scallops for corners. The kitchen was also sprayed ashy white, although two weeks earlier Harry had written to the Housing Office asking that it be painted its former bright yellow and offering to buy and deliver the paint.

All these details registered, but didn't reach deeply. There was something far more penetrating. I had grown used to visiting the apartment in its damaged state; it had looked dreadful but its debris was ours, laden with history. There were light squares on the grayed walls where our pictures had hung, and light circles on the blackened floors where our chairs had stood. We had seen the world from its huge old windows with their elaborately molded frames. But this place was alien, blank, nobody's. Smaller without the furniture. It was like the first day I arrived there twenty years ago, pregnant, only then we had set to work to make it a place we could live in. It had had a future. This place didn't even seem to have a past. It did not seem possible that this was the place where I had sat, heavy with our first child, watching far across the river the lights of the roller coaster of Palisades Amusement Park, itself now vanished. But if not here, where?

November 6, 1984. Election Day. I went back to the old block this morning to vote, but barely glanced at the building as I passed. At the polls, as I expected, I met a couple of my old neighbors—Nena O'Neill on line, Coula Lurier checking registrations as usual. Afterwards I shopped at our old fruit market on Broadway; the Korean woman asked where I had been all this time. November 6 and still not back. Six days late. Is it worth protesting, we wonder, or would that prove us to have grown petty and unduly suspicious? Word from Columbia has it that the delay is caused by Con Edison—something about wiring, permits.

Thanksgiving weekend. Twenty-four days late, but Harry has had word from Len Lerner that the apartments are ready to be occupied. He goes to the building, but Mrs. Flanagan does not have our keys, nor does she know where they are. She will try to have them on Monday. Already people are beginning to telephone Harry to complain about their paint jobs and linoleum: Why didn't they treat us like human beings, ask us to come in and choose . . . ? Harry wearily says he'll call Len Lerner to see if anything can be done. . . .

And early in December the tenants gather as they used to on a Thursday evening in Kenny Schaeffer's office. Nena O'Neill is not there—she will remain in her downtown office. Jerry and Selma Silverstein are not there. They have bought a small co-op apartment in midtown Manhattan. Of the rest, only Diana Angel is back in 547. The others are hesitant, afraid that moving back and beginning to pay rent would signify their acceptance of the unacceptable restoration. For as the discussion begins, it emerges that the cheap paint is already peeling in places, there are holes in floors, the toilets are smoke-stained, there are no shower curtain rods, some baseboard electrical outlets have been painted over (in our apartment, a full-length mirror was sprayed white), furniture stored by Columbia during the restoration has not reappeared. As for the public areas, the basement storage room is gone; the elevator is deplorable; no one has yet been given a mailbox key and mail lies on a table in the lobby. . . . Armed with lists of the problems, the tenants, along with Kenny Schaeffer, will visit the appropriate Columbia official to urge that they be rectified.

At Columbia's Low Library in this fall of 1984, the Dalai Lama, in exile from Tibet, addressed a crowd of one thousand people on Buddhism and its techniques for learning and practicing compassion. "It may be boring for you," he said, "always hearing 'compassion, compassion' from the Dalai Lama's mouth. To sustain the body, you have to eat every day. Compassion is like bread, you always need it. You can't say, 'too much bread.' "

University president Michael Sovern, later asked if he "hit it off" with the Dalai Lama, replied, "How could you not? We all feel kinder and more compassionate."

Appendix

On March 2, 1984, I wrote to Larry Dais, director of community affairs:

Dear Mr. Dais,

You suggested, when I called on Friday to ask if I might speak with you about the events surrounding the March 2, 1983, fire at 547 Riverside Drive, that I send you a list of questions which you would either answer in writing or refer to the appropriate Columbia officials for a reply. As you remember, my questions were for an article or possibly longer work which I hope to write about the fire, the legal complexities it engendered, and the effects on the tenants' lives. (Just to establish my credentials, I have published three novels with Harper & Row, in 1980, 1981, and 1983, and have a book of stories coming out with them in August; I have also written numerous reviews and articles on the arts for major national magazines and papers, and have taught writing at several universities, including Columbia.) My purpose in contacting you was to have as many facts as possible at my disposal, and to give Columbia a fair chance to state its position, so that my writing can be as fully informed and close to the truth as possible.

The following questions are somewhat more formal than those that would have come out in conversation with you. In any case, here they are:

1. What were you empowered or instructed to tell the tenants

about the fate of the building, during the first meetings with them after the fire?

2. Several tenants have mentioned that after these first few meetings with Columbia representatives in the days immediately following the fire, the university refused to meet with them or to answer their questions about plans for the building. Why did it refuse?

3. Who was in charge of planning the future of the building and deciding what to do about its tenants?

4. What did Columbia hope to do with the building, assuming it was not constrained by the courts? Did Columbia's plans (I don't mean architectural or structural plans) for the building change between March 2 and August 26, when the court rendered its decision? If so, how?

5. Would Columbia have preferred to have tenants remain in the temporary housing it provided in a few cases, and was this why it offered temporary housing at one point?

6. What was Columbia's attitude towards the tenants' demands for restoration of the building? I get the impression from my inquiries so far that Columbia regarded this group of tenants as particularly intractable, and wondered if you would like to confirm or deny, or modify that impression in any way.

7. The fire marshal's report stated that the June 8 fire at 547 Riverside Drive was arson. Has Columbia conducted any investigation to discover the culprit?

8. As you may remember, between mid-April and the first week in June, Columbia and the tenants attempted to reach an agreement, but these negotiations broke down when Columbia refused to set a date for completion of the north wing, and tenants refused to sign without such a date. Why did Columbia refuse to say when it would finish rebuilding the north wing?

I would be sincerely grateful to have your answers, or the answers of any of your colleagues who were more closely involved in the matter. Again, I am asking in the interest of thoroughness and truth. If you or any of your colleagues would like to discuss these or related matters, I would be more than willing to meet with you. Thank you.

Sincerely yours,
[signed] Lynne Sharon Schwartz

Three weeks later I received a reply from Larry Dais thanking me for my letter of inquiry but stating that "in light of the current litigation" it would be unwise to discuss the fire "at this time."

The ligitation referred to is the negligence suit brought by several of the tenants against Columbia. At the time of this correspondence the suit was in a dormant state; only in the summer of 1984 did Columbia begin the preliminary step of taking depositions, a process that seems likely to continue well into 1985.

On April 3, 1984, I received a phone call, regarding my letter to Larry Dais, from Lloyd Kaplan, representing Columbia University for Howard J. Rubenstein Associates, a public relations firm. Kaplan said that since I was involved in a lawsuit with Columbia, I wasn't in the best position to write an account of the fire, and moreover that it was not usual for Columbia representatives to talk with someone involved in a lawsuit. Kaplan suggested I consult my attorney about withdrawing from the suit, but added that he couldn't guarantee even then that my questions would be answered.

At the urging of tenants and their attorneys, the damaged and then shoddily fixed apartments in 547 Riverside Drive were eventually renovated again, with much better results. By March of 1985, more than a year after the agreement with Columbia was signed, and two years after the fire, the apartments were ready to be reoccupied, and people began moving back in.

During the two years following the March 1983 Final Report by the Columbia Senate Panel on Housing and Rental Policy, Columbia increased its efforts to convert Morningside Heights apartments to institutional uses. In response, during the spring of 1985, the Coalition of Tenants of Non-Profit Institutional Landlords launched a campaign to support proposed legislation that would protect tenants' rights to their homes, including rallies, leafletting, and lobbying of state legislators, and culminating in a demonstration at the state capitol in Albany on June 5 and 6.